Sometimes the Bull Wins

BY JIM WILLOUGHBY

WitWorks™

DEDICATION

To my wife, Sue, without whom none of this would be.

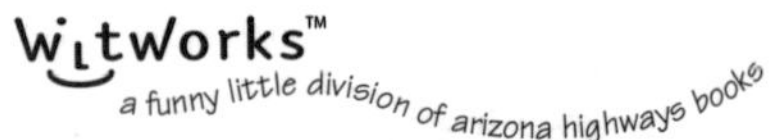

2039 West Lewis Avenue, Phoenix, Arizona 85009
Telephone: (602) 712-2200
Web site: www.witworksbooks.com

Publisher – Win Holden
Managing Editor – Bob Albano
Associate Editor – Evelyn Howell
Associate Editor – PK Perkin McMahon
Art Director – Mary Winkelman Velgos
Photography Director – Peter Ensenberger
Production Director – Cindy Mackey
Production Coordinator – Kim Ensenberger

Library of Congress Catalog Number: 2001097743
ISBN 1-893860-81-7

FIRST EDITION, published in 2002.
Printed in the United States.

Cover design – Mary Winkelman Velgos
Book design – Beth Anderson

FOREWARD

I had heard of will-o-the-wisp, but until I moved to Arizona, I had never heard of Will-o-BEE. Now, I'm happy to report that this Jim Will-o-bee (who apparently doesn't know how to spell) has been busy as a bee turning out a honey of a book! And there is nothing wispy about it. It is very big on humor and strong on cartoon art.

Billy, Dolly, Jeffy, and PJ, in my newspaper feature, may not understand all the satire and plays on words, but they'll love the loose, appealing drawings. To them an outhouse is the Toys-R-Us plastic play-cottage in the back-yard. However, they'll learn easily, through this book, that an outhouse is the outdoor potty which obviously was prevalent when Willoughby was a kid. But, since he grew up in Canada, it must have been called an "oathouse."

We also learn herein about cowboys, rodeos, saloons, and the Wild West. So, you see, the book is highly educational as well as entertaining.

I'm glad I had the chance to peruse this Western treasury before the rest of my family got their grubby hands on it.

Although, as a competing cartoonist, I hate to admit it, Jim Willoughby's many years of experience with pen and ink stands out brilliantly in his art. I sure wish he'd retire sometime during this millennium.

Bil Keane
Creator of *The Family Circus*

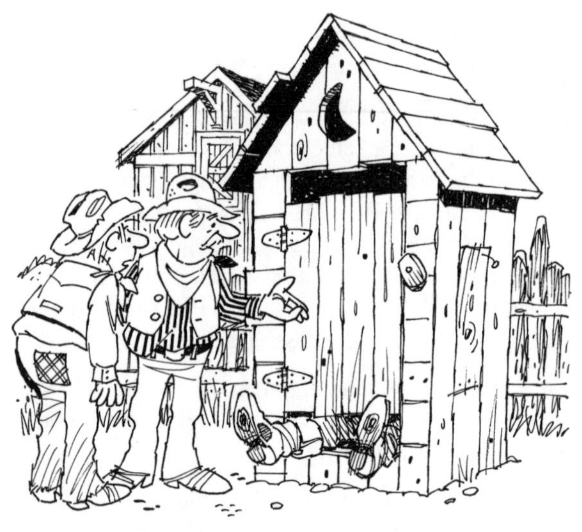

"Maybe we better check on Ellsworth."

TABLE OF CONTENTS

The Cowboy Life 6

How's the Plumbing? 28

Ride 'em, Gran'ma 48

The Swinging Doors 60

"Hi, Doc, How Am I?" 70

Sheep in the Meadow,
Cows in the Corn 86

Don't Become a Cowboy If... 100

View From the Pew 106

Don't Ever... 122

Too Much Tabasco? 128

It Was the Judge 138

The Cowboy Life

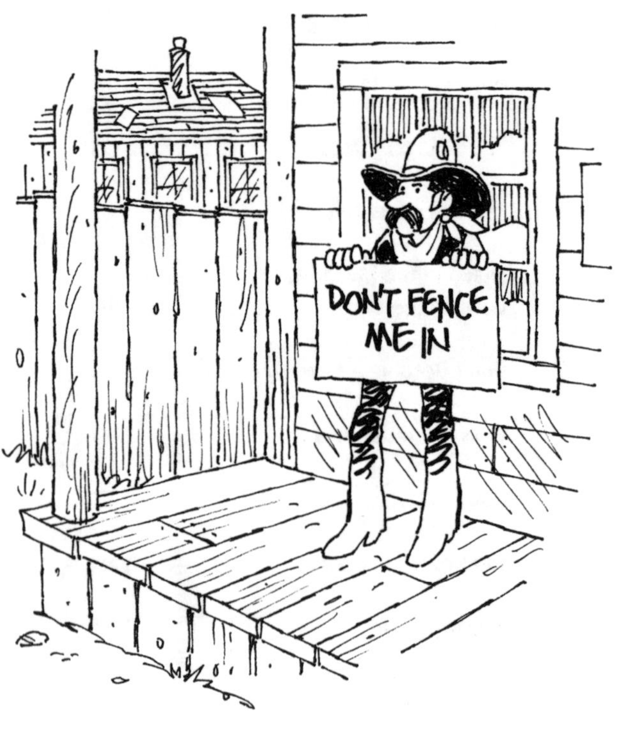

A wealthy rancher out of Ruidoso is said to have had several thousand dollars on him at any given time.

Out West, that's what we call keeping good company.

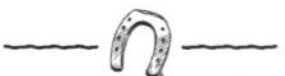

Bragging about the new horse he had acquired, a cowboy told his friend, "He can turn on a dime."

"Great!" his friend responded. "I wonder what he could do on a quarter."

I asked this horse expert what I could do to get more speed out my horse.

"Lose 40 pounds," he told me.

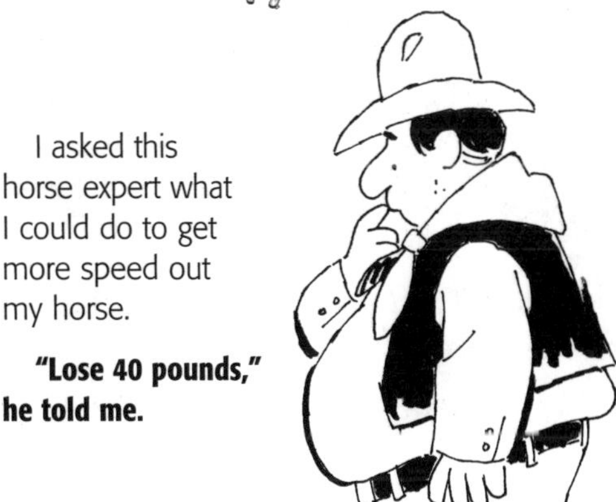

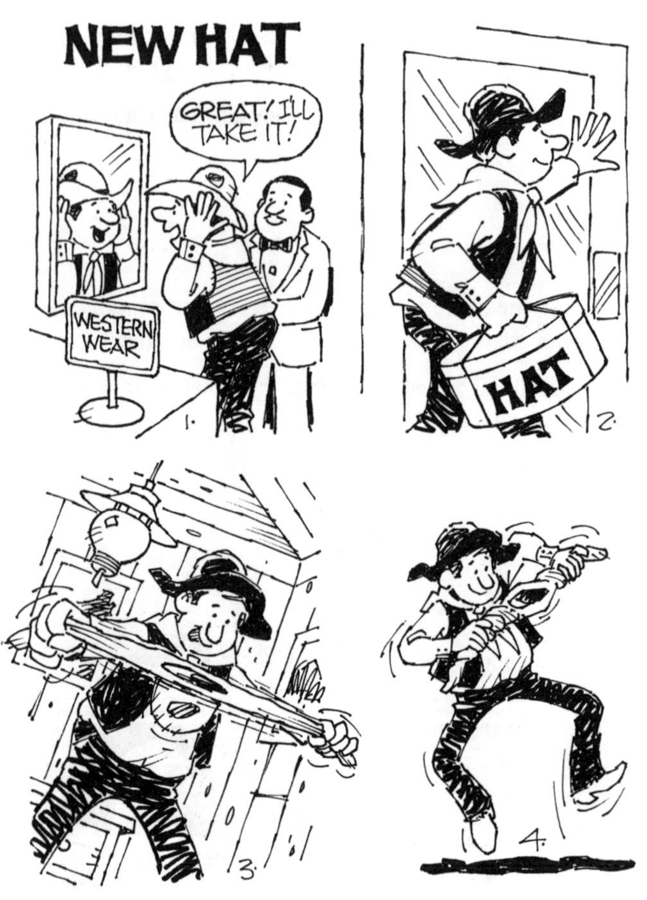
NEW HAT
GREAT! I'LL TAKE IT!
WESTERN WEAR
1.
HAT
2.
3.
4.

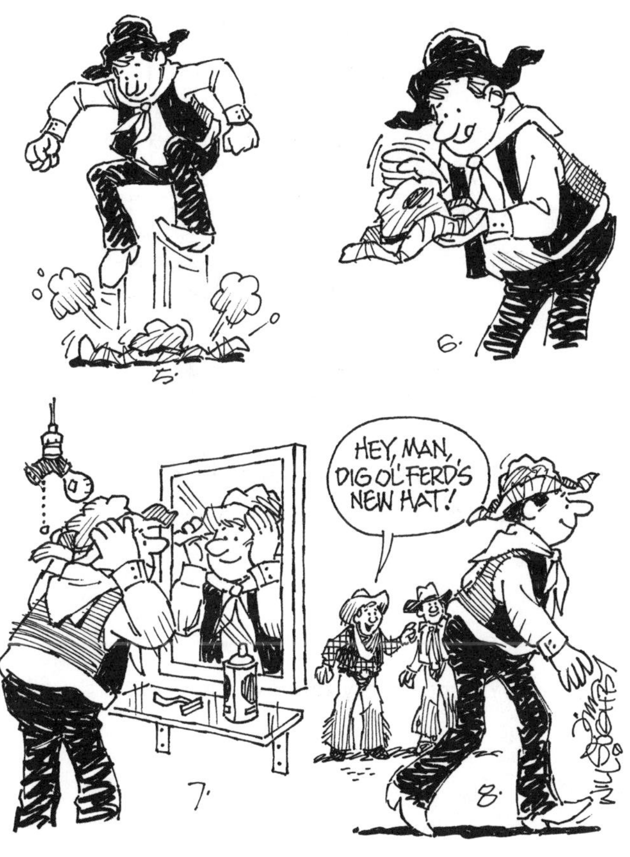
5.
6.
7.
HEY, MAN,
DIG OL' FERD'S
NEW HAT!
8.

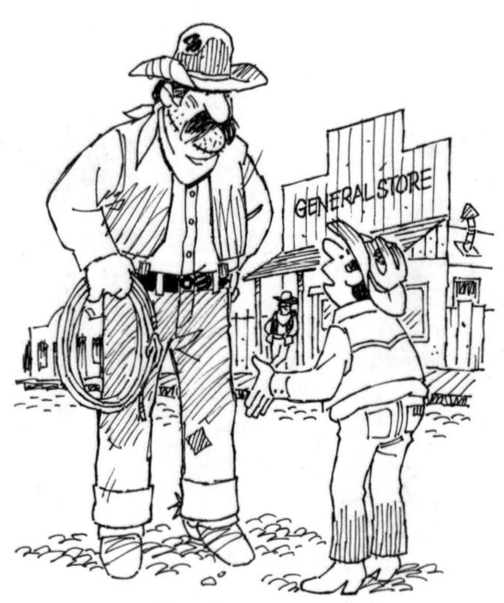

"How else are Arizona cowboys different from other cowboys?"

An apple a day **ain't very much pay.**

A really good buddy is one who is always there for you **even if he doesn't like you.**

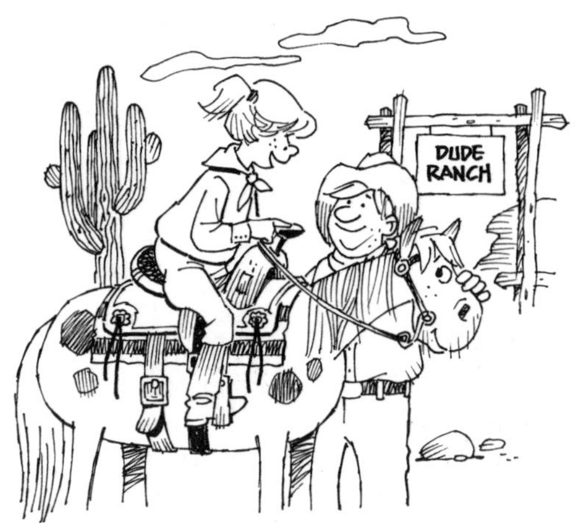

"Is this the gear shift?"

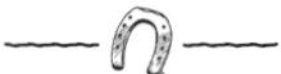

A genuine cowboy must be able to ride a horse.

Merry-go-round horses don't count.

——∩——

A young girl enrolled in a riding class at a dude ranch. When her horse got galloping too fast for her, she asked the handsome cowboy beside her, **"Where's the brake pedal?"**

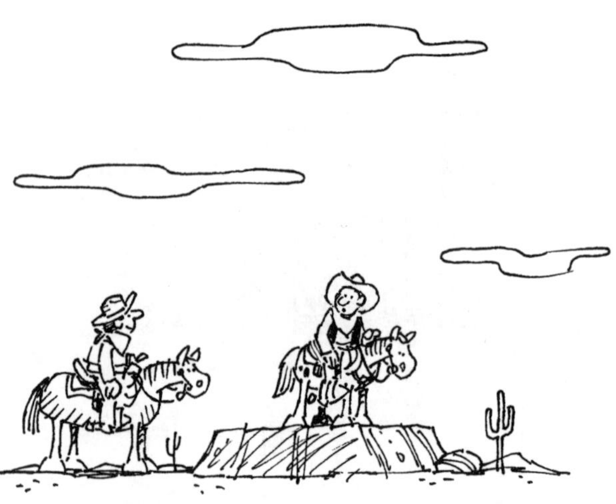

"You get a better view from up here, Sully."

Rocking leisurely back and forth on the front porch, the old-timer told his visitor, "I used to travel a good bit, but **riding the 3 miles into town eventually got to be too much for me."**

The good thing about horses as compared to cars is that you don't have to **lube them or change the oil.**

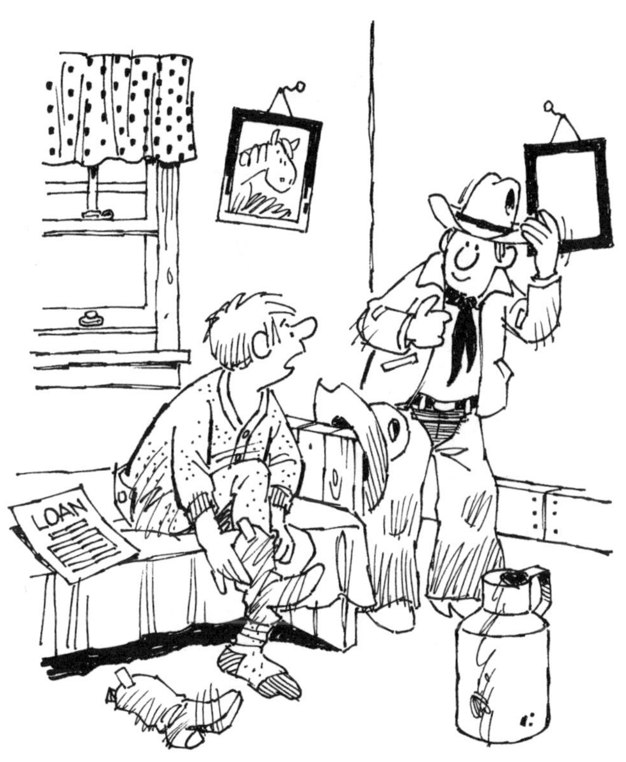

"I listed you as a reference, and they threw me out of the bank."

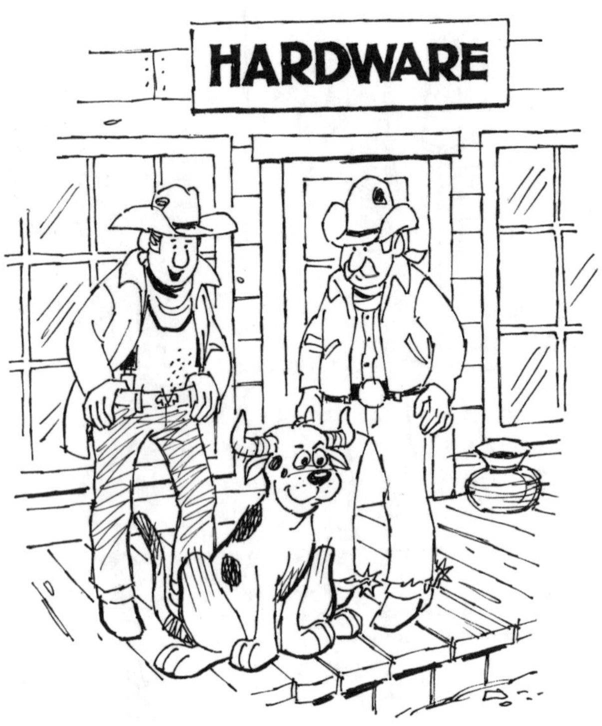

"He's the best darn cow dog I ever had."

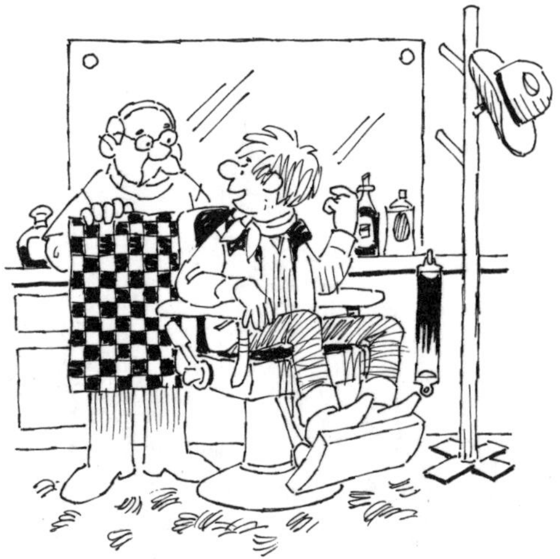

"Make it look like Clint Eastwood."

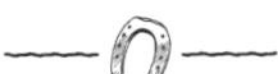

Burro, mule, jackass, javelina breath—whatever you call them, they'll still be ornery.

That's why some muleskinners call them names that ain't fit to print!

Think twice before taking a shortcut **through a stampeding herd of buffalo.**

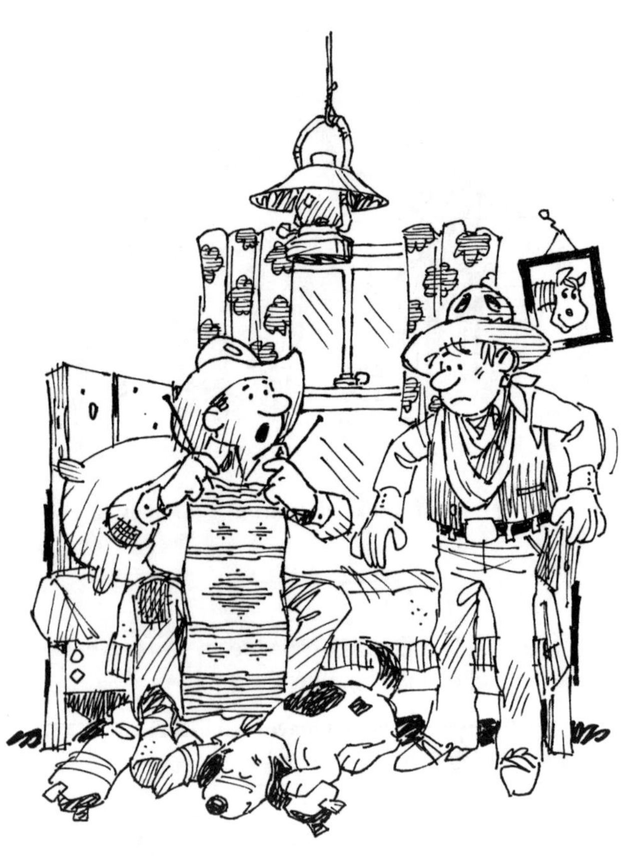

"Everybody should have a hobby, Ferd."

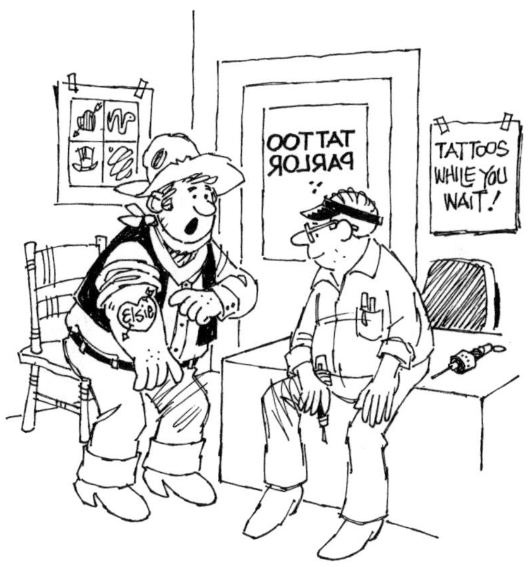

"I'd like it changed to 'Sue.'"

There is a classic movie scene with a cowboy riding into the sunset . . .

But they shot the scene early in the morning!

Why are they called cowboys when **it's horses they ride?**

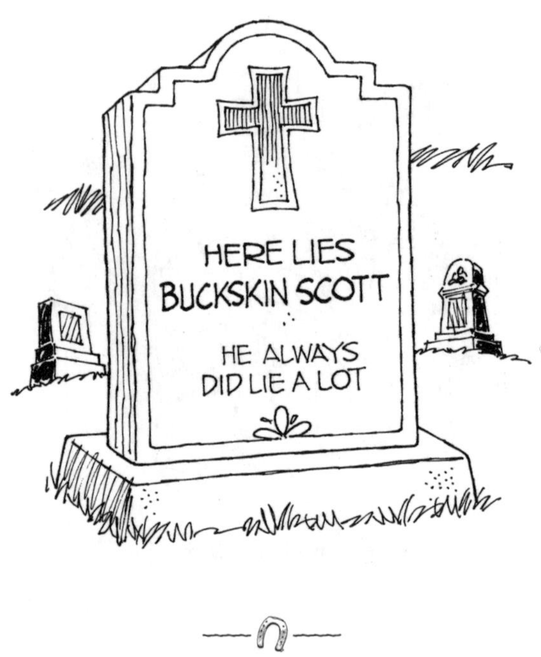

Cowboy hats have many uses, **including being worn on the head.**

It's so quiet on the prairie at night, you have to pinch yourself occasionally **to be sure you're there.**

There are so many, many miles of fence to fix on Freeland's ranch that he gets **WIRED** just thinking about it!

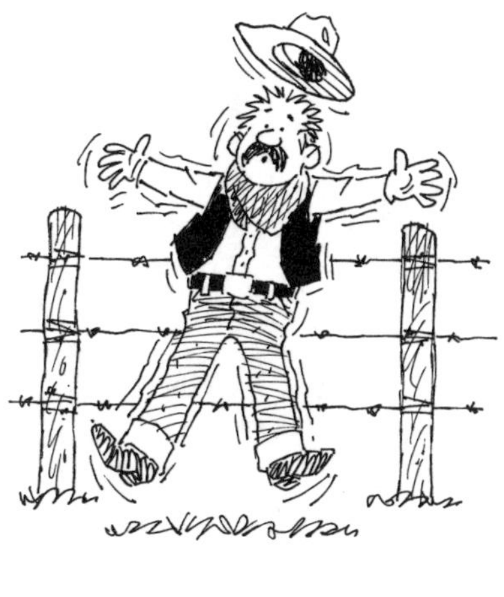

Bigger ain't necessarily better . . .

. . . Unless you're talking bank accounts.

Someone hollered, "FIRE!" And all heads turned toward the bunkhouse. Sure enough, flames were shooting out from under the door. A fire brigade line was quickly formed from the well to the house, and water splashed abundantly.

That was the closest those boys have been to taking a bath in months.

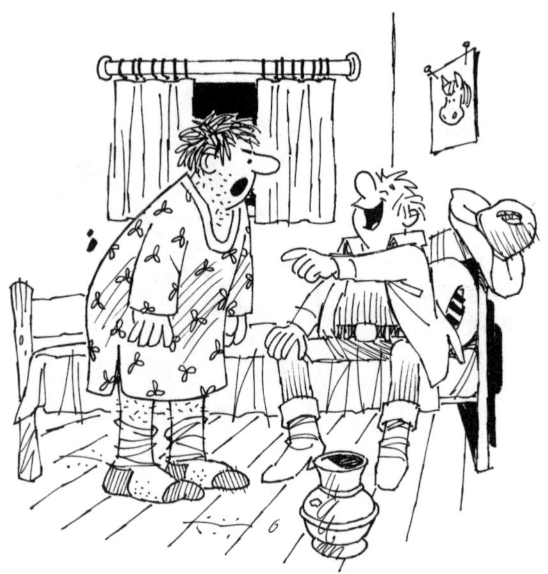

"What's so funny about a nightgown?"

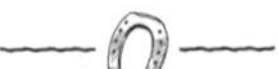

Be an animal advocate—**take a cow out to lunch.**

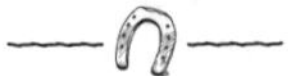

Trying to be pals with the bank's loan officer is like trying to **court a rattlesnake.**

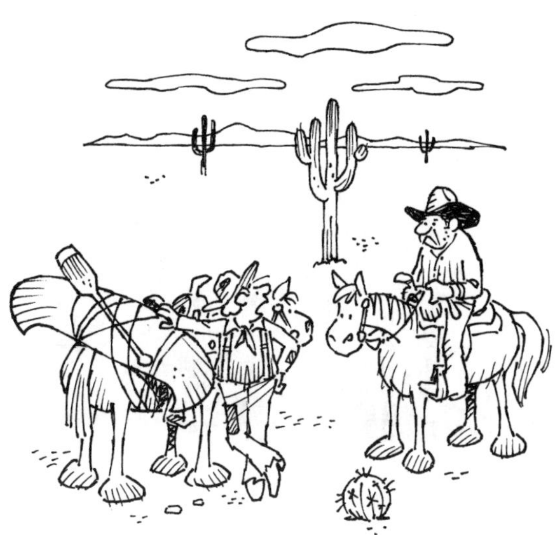

"I understand when it rains out here, it really rains!"

A real cowboy doesn't climb the highest mountain.

He goes around it.

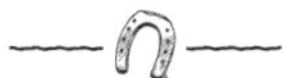

Rounding up stray cattle **don't leave much time for fishin'.**

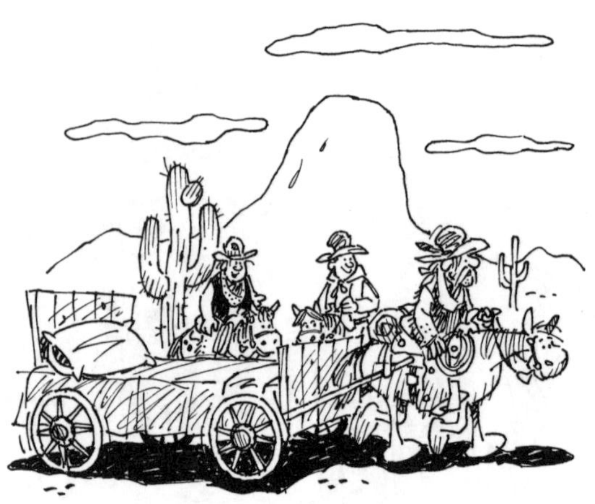

"Ragsdale likes the comforts."

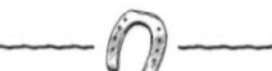

We knew this cowboy who could throw a rope a country mile . . .

. . . But he couldn't find one that long.

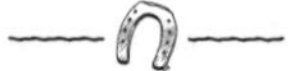

Bucky Blaner builds a fence you can't get under, through, or over.

That makes it tough when the bull you're after is on the other side.

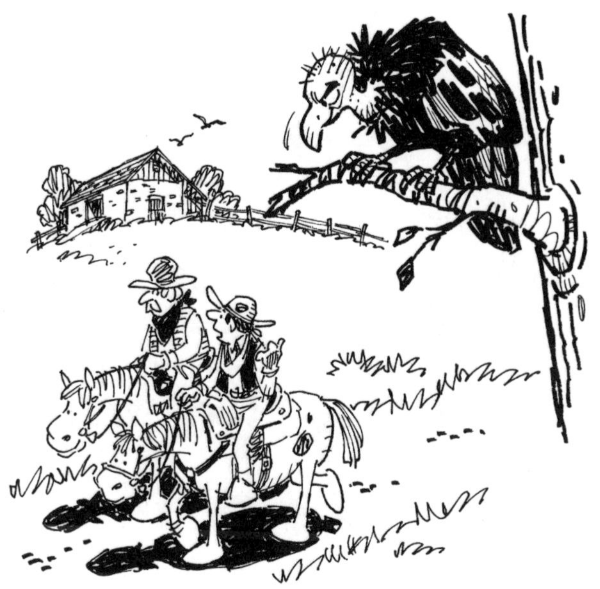

"Duane, are you feeling OK?"

If it can't be done from atop a horse, **it ain't worth doing.**

Buckskin Ruffner has been riding horses so long, he **forgot how to walk.**

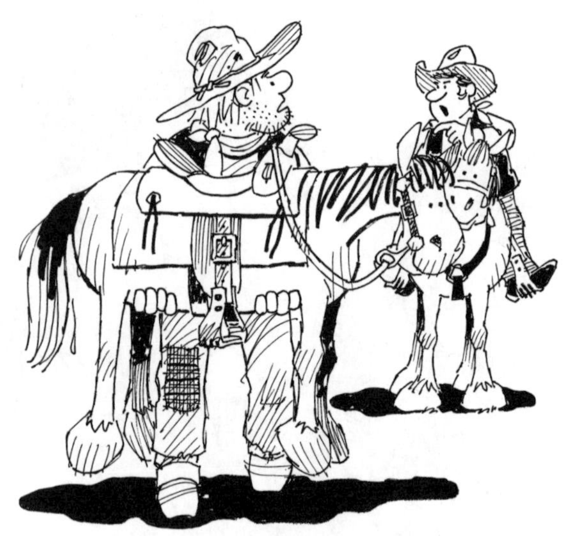

"No, no, Kallmeyer, you're supposed to ride the horse!"

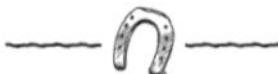

The covered wagon was our **first sports utility vehicle.**

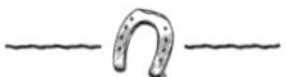

Buzzards don't make good **traveling companions.**

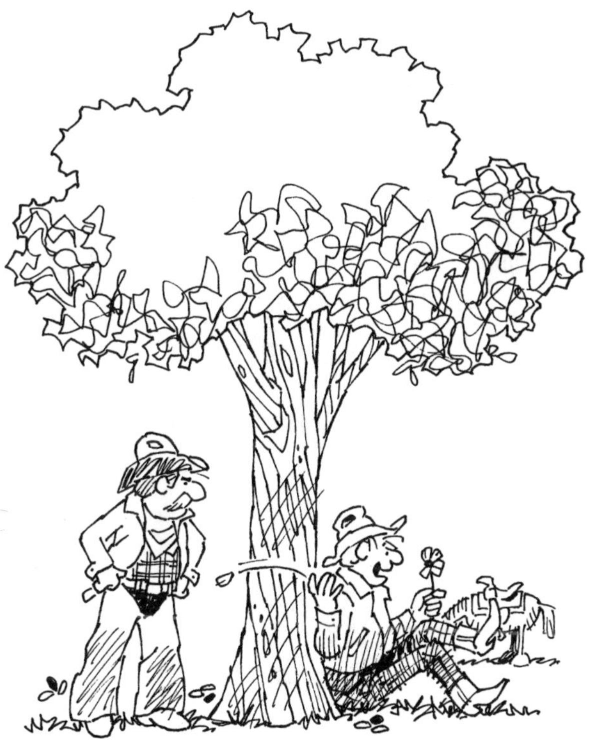

"She loves me, she loves me not..."

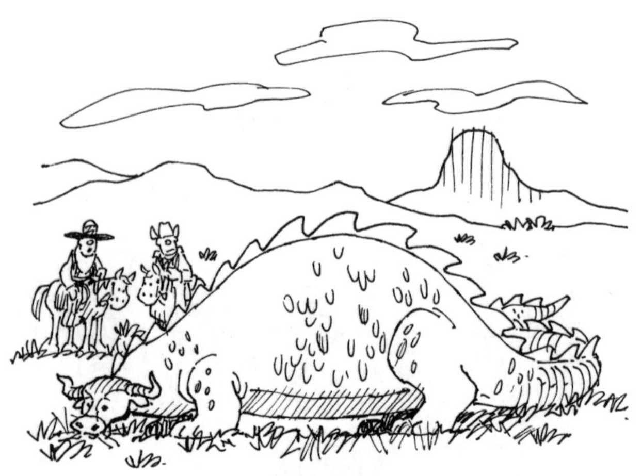

"Someone in the laboratory has been clowning around again."

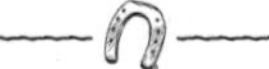

Everything about Texas is big . . .

. . . Especially its ego.

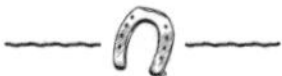

You can't get lost out West . . .

. . . Any way you go is spectacular.

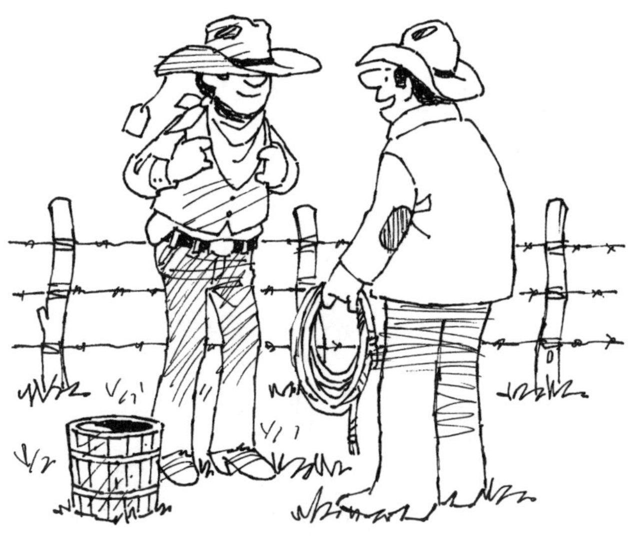

"Other than that, though, it's a nifty hat, Monty."

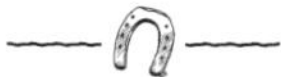

Lady friend: "What's that peculiar fragrance you're wearing?"

Cowboy: "Cologne de Cow Pie."

How's the Plumbing?

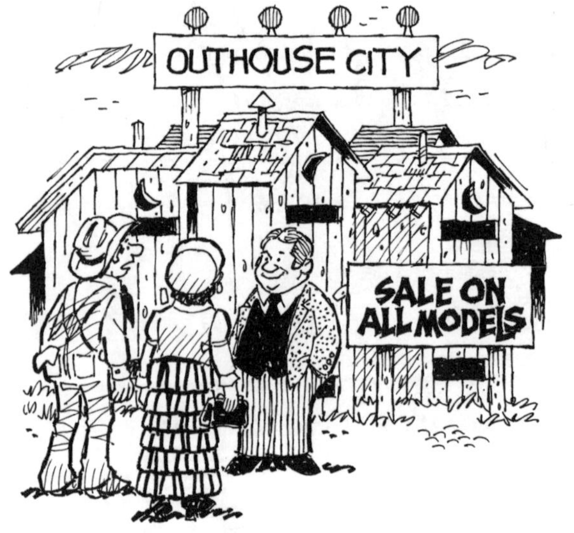

It is doubtful that the history of the outhouse goes as far back as the Garden of Eden, but this ignoble edifice ranks high on anyone's list of historic places. And rightly so. Pioneers in the old West put up an outhouse before even starting work on their living quarters, being careful to place the structure with the familiar quarter-moon cutout on the door well downwind.

Outhouses were sometimes fondly dubbed with the names of cherished relatives or friends. In polite conversation, a cowhand might be heard to say to his bunkmates, "If you gentlemen will excuse me, I'm goin' out and pay a visit to Aunt Bertha."

These legendary shanties most often were constructed with one hole in them, giving the occupant a degree of privacy. A large household, however, might set up two or even three holes. However many, the outhouse played a serious role in the lives

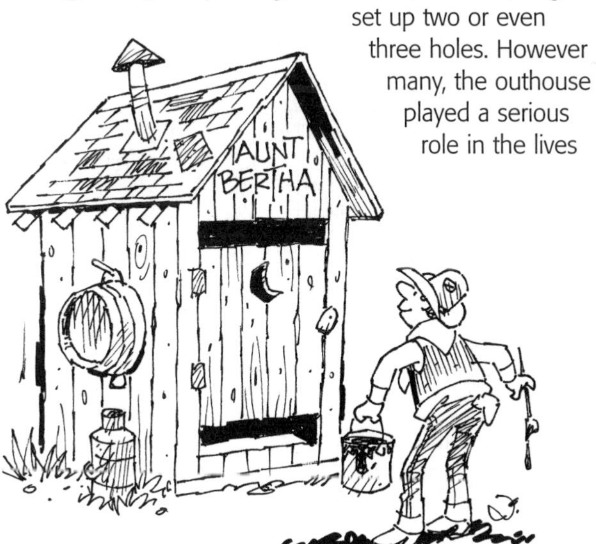

of our hardy ancestors. Still, it was often the butt (no pun intended!) of pranks and jokes. Kids delighted in pushing them over, often with an irate occupant inside.

We like Sherman Payne's story of two bored gas station guys in sparsely populated Salome, the little Arizona desert town made famous by the writings of humorist Dick Wick Hall. Figuring to liven things up, the two wired

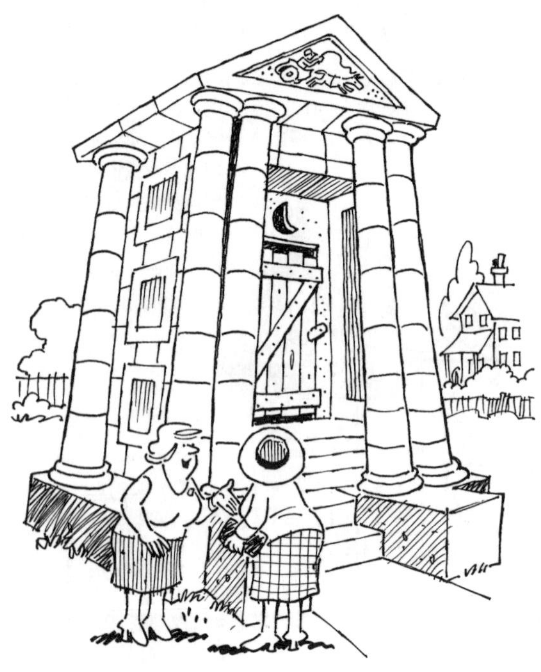

"Reginald always does things up big."

up a one-way communication system from the gas station to underneath the seats of the two-holer out back.

No sooner had they finished rigging it up when a posh Cadillac spun in off the highway and parked beside the pumps. A sophisticated lady stepped out, instructed the two fellows to fill it up and clean the windows. Then she made her way to the outhouse.

While one guy tended to the car's needs, the other—giving the lady ample time to get comfortably adjusted—spoke into the jury-rigged microphone, **"Would you move over to the other seat, lady? We're painting down here."**

Seconds later, the frazzled-looking lady reappeared, paid her tab, and sped off in the Cadillac.

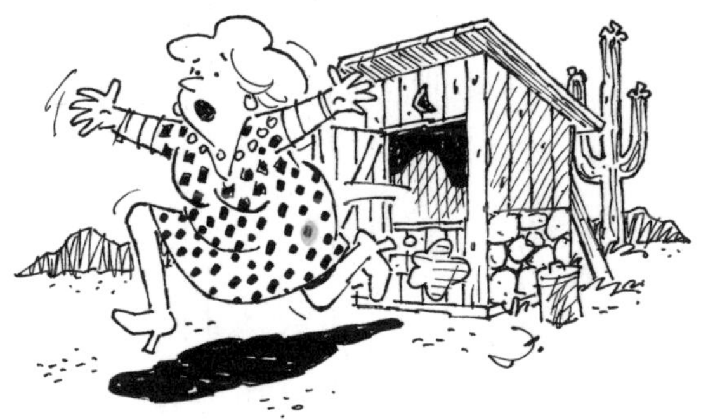

This chapter treats outhouses on the lighter side and will hopefully recall some of the reader's own experiences with this novel bit of early-American architecture.

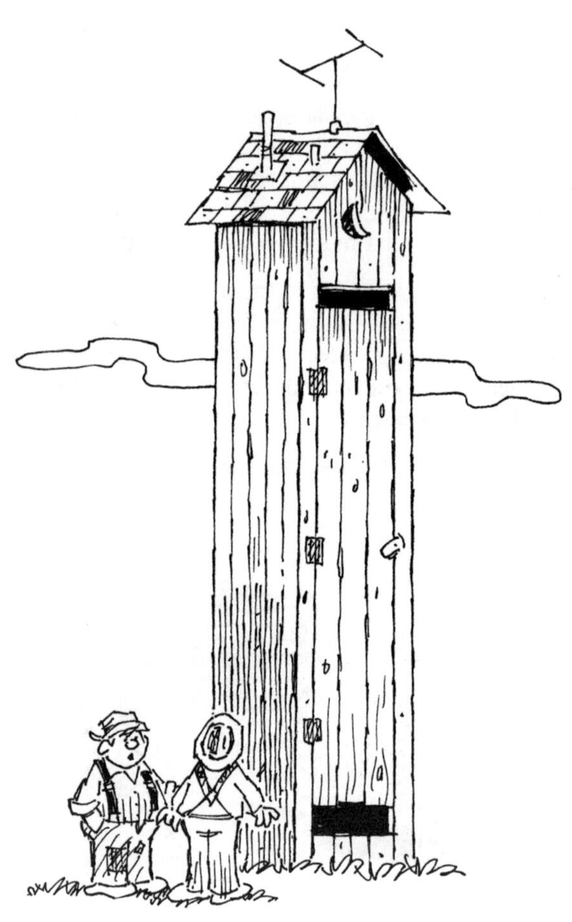

"It was previously owned by a Lakers basketball player."

An outhouse salesperson we know compiled the 10 dumbest questions asked by couples buying their first outhouse.

10. Do you have something with a **washer and dryer**?

9. How are the **acoustics**? I sing in the shower.

8. Does it have a **phone**?

7. Is it **carpeted**?

6. Do you have something with a **linen closet**?

5. How about **curtains**?

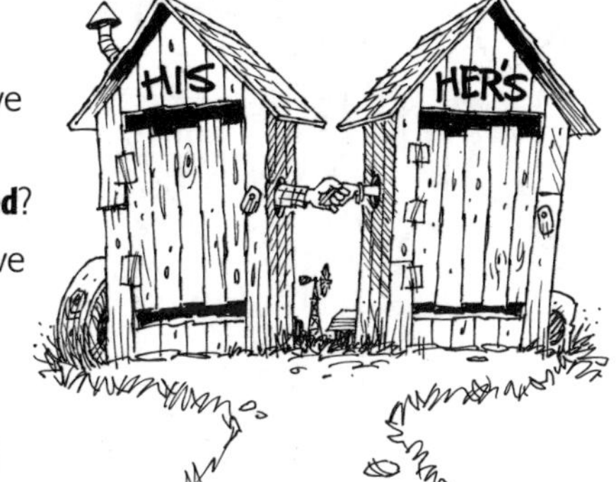

4. Are all the features **color coordinated**?

3. Could we get one with **patio doors** in the back?

2. Do you have anything with a **skylight**?

1. Where do you keep the **toilet bowl brush**?

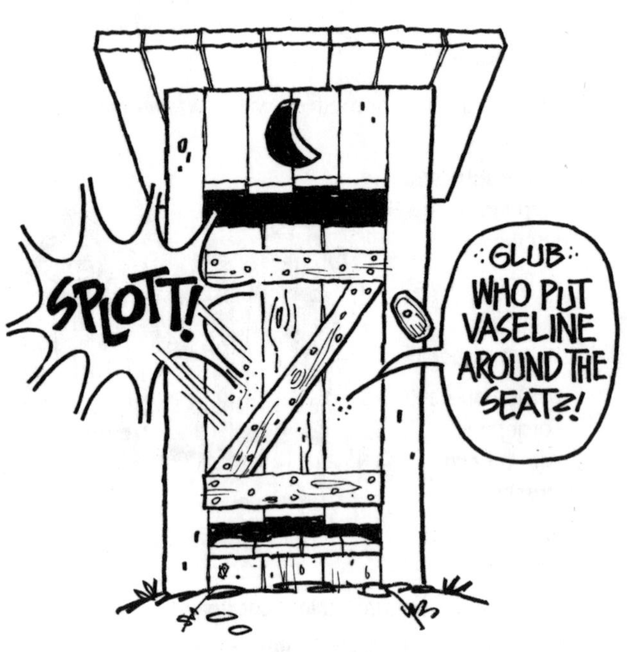
SPLOTT!
GLUB
WHO PUT VASELINE AROUND THE SEAT?!

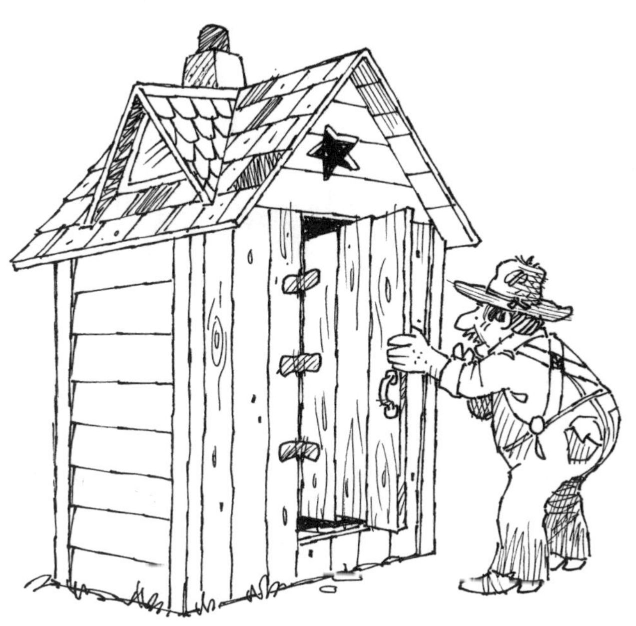

"Gosh, I'm sorry, ma'am.
I thought this was a phone booth."

How long
a minute is
depends on
**which side of
the outhouse
door you're on.**

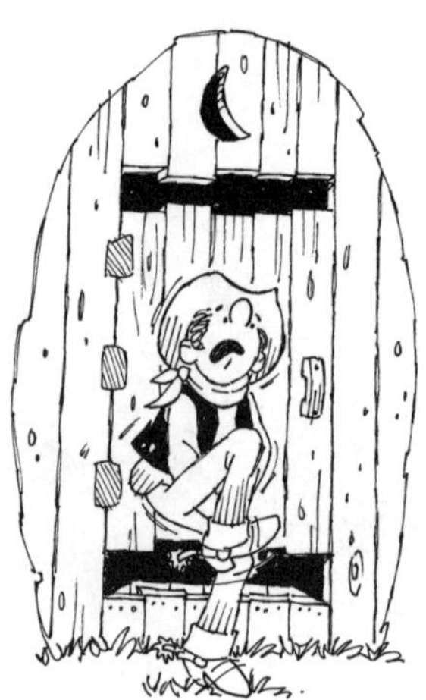

The middle of the night is no time to have to go,

Especially if it's snowing out
and 20 degrees below.

I timed it right, got there on time,

And then found out, it costs a dime.

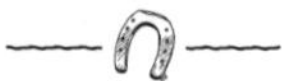

There's nothing appealing about an outhouse . . .

. . . Unless you need to use one.

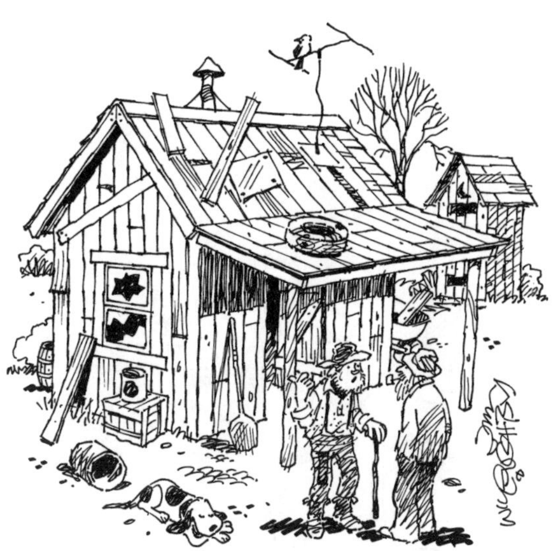

"I bin gonna paint it for twenny years, but I can't decide what color."

Cowhand's voice from inside the outhouse:

"Hey, Ma, we're out of catalog!"

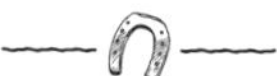

A royal flush **has nothing to do with an outhouse.**

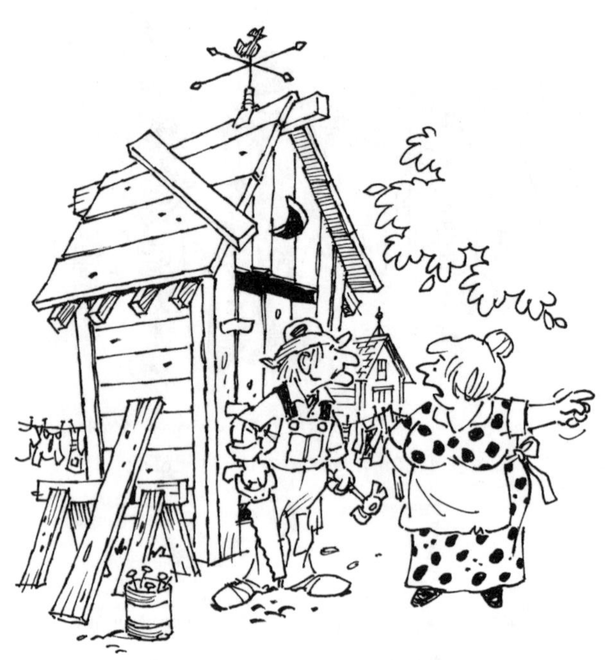

"I think I'd like it better over there."

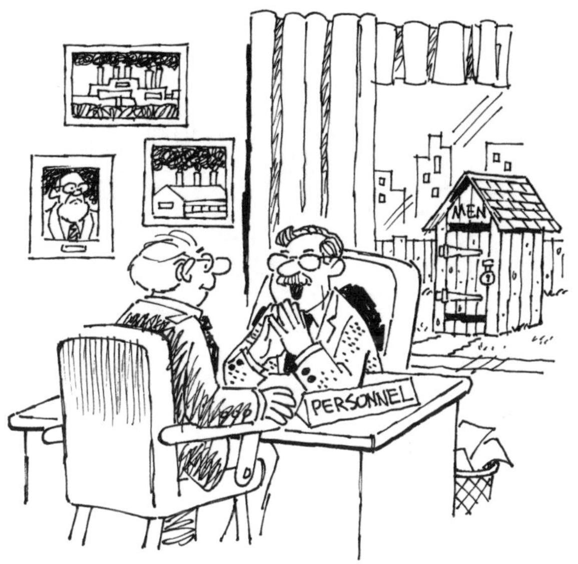

"And, of course, you'll have your own key to the executive men's room."

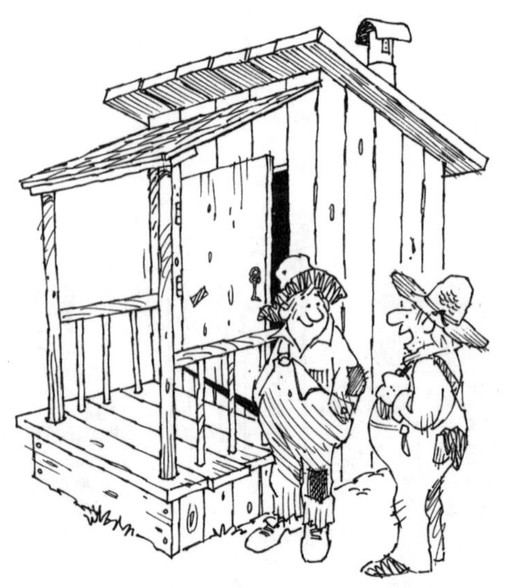

"By golly, you're right. You don't see many with a front porch on 'em."

Our privy was so far from the house, by the time we got back from it, **we had to go again.**

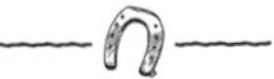

Our neighbors painted their outhouse a bright red, and **a raging bull knocked it into the next county.**

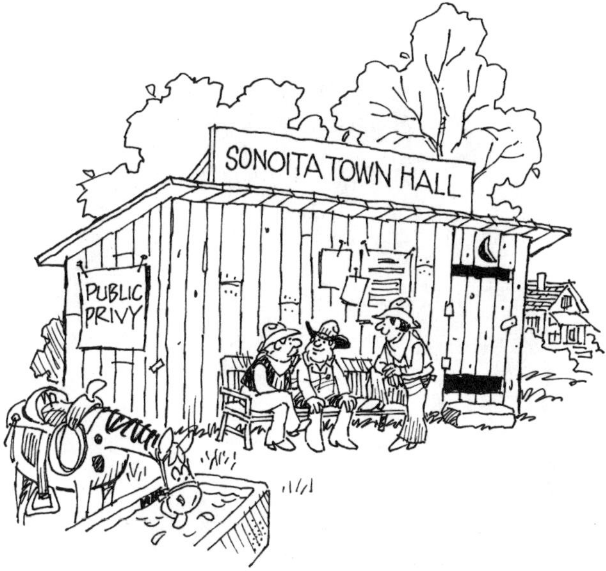

We know a town in Arizona that built a deluxe 17-seater.

It also served as the village's town hall and meeting place.

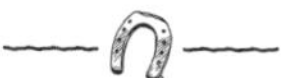

The town's richest family had an outhouse so big, **a family of seven asked if they could lease it.**

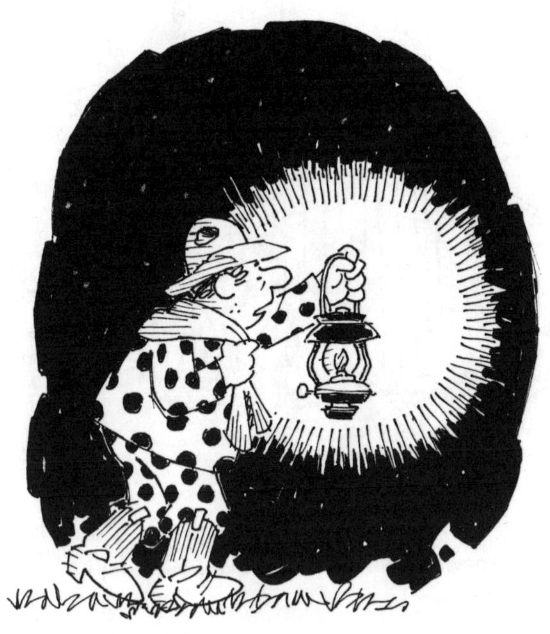

I remember a party one night when Pa headed for the outhouse.

I don't know which was lit up the most – Pa or his coal-oil lantern.

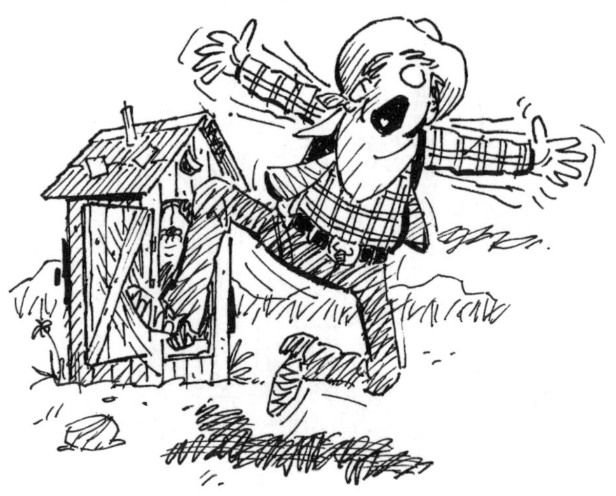

Sitting in the privy, waiting for something to happen,
Along came a black widow spider.
If I had wings,
They'd be a flappin!

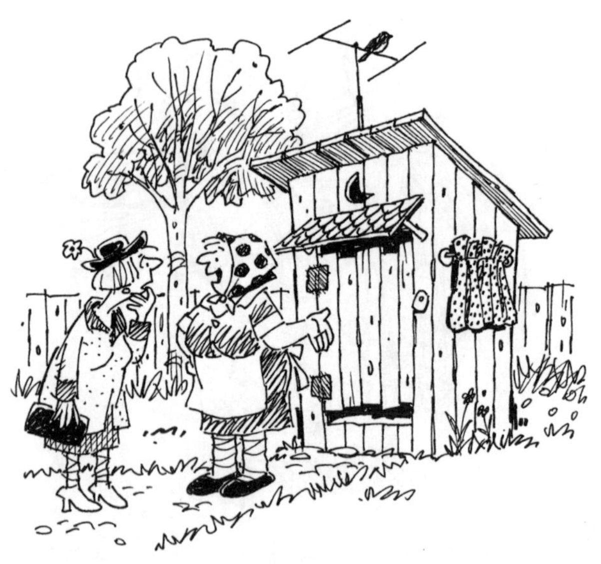

"We made it over into a guest room."

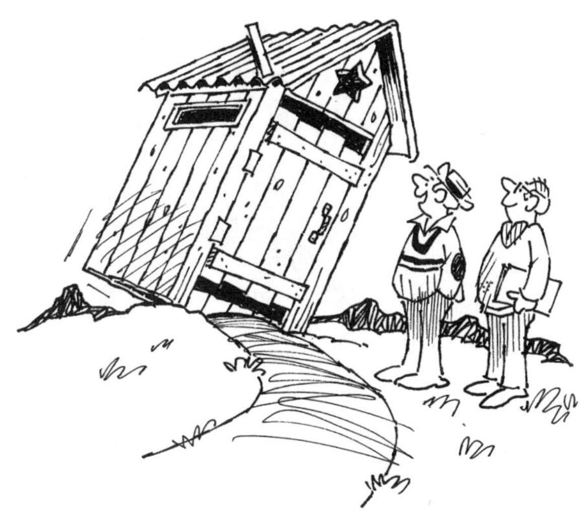

"Locals fondly refer to it as 'the leaning tower of Hog Hollow'."

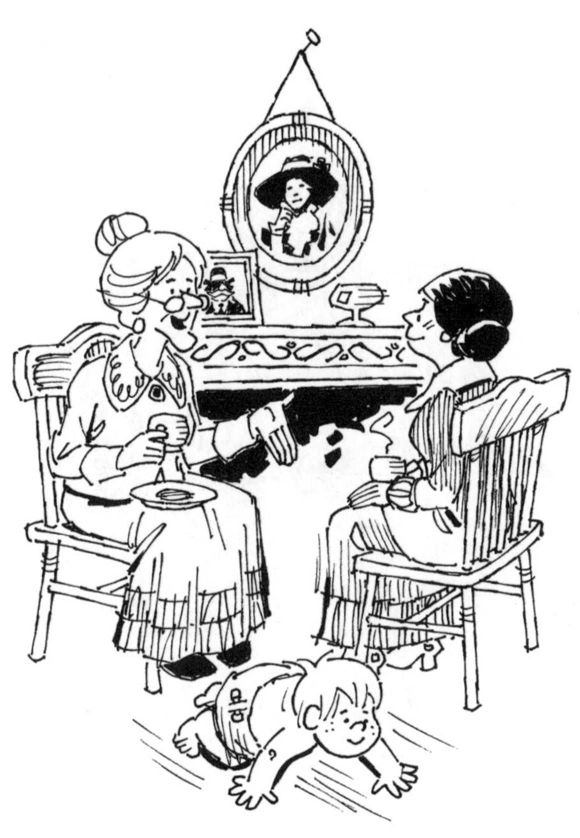

"Is he outhouse trained, yet?"

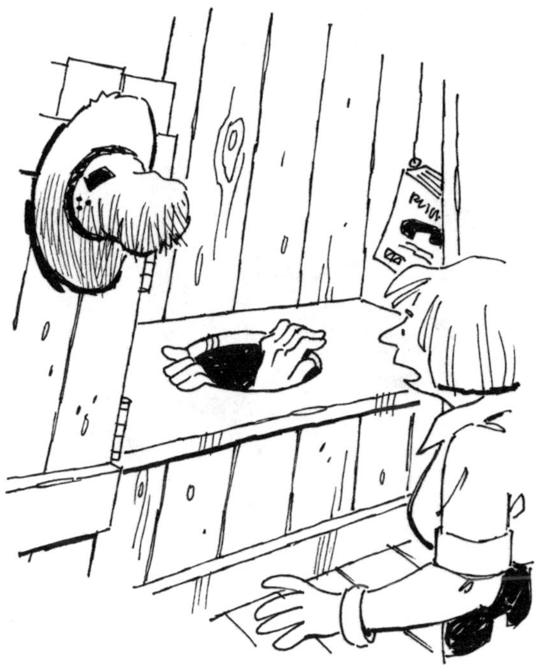

"You've got to put on more weight, Paw!"

Ride 'em, Gran'ma

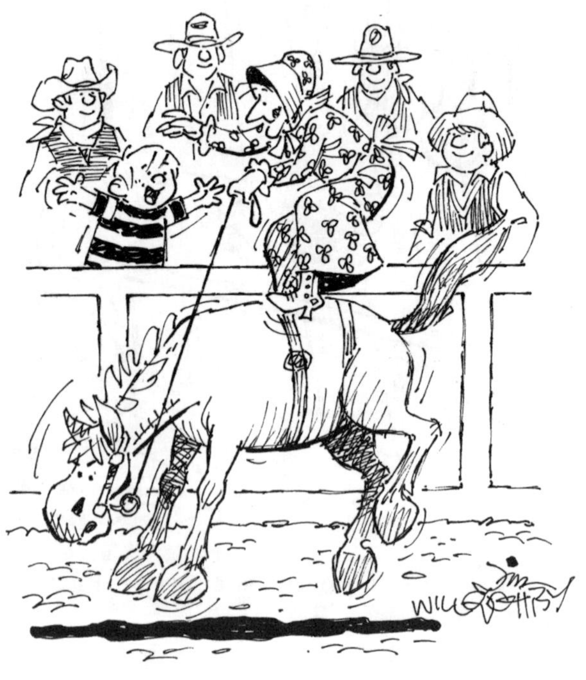

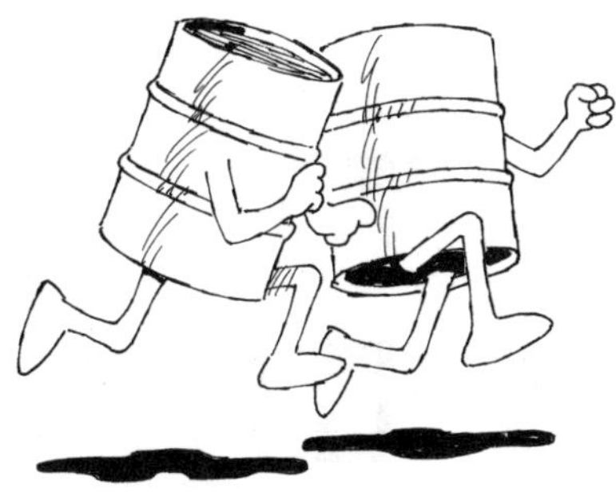

Barrel racing is a popular rodeo event . . .

But we have never known anyone who has **seen barrels race.**

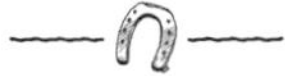

In rodeo jargon, chaps don't refer to **bonny Englishmen.**

—∩—

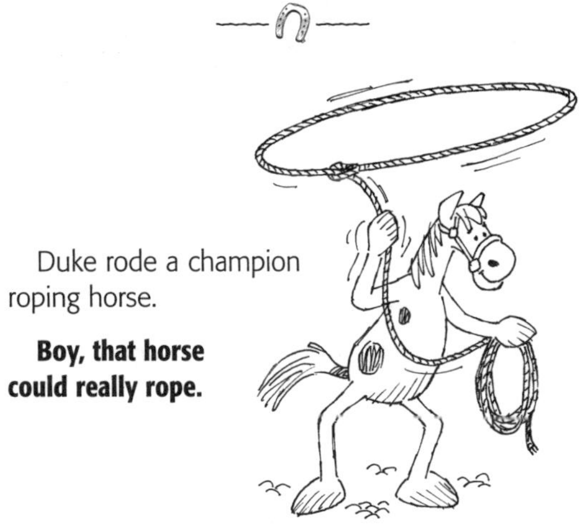

Duke rode a champion roping horse.

Boy, that horse could really rope.

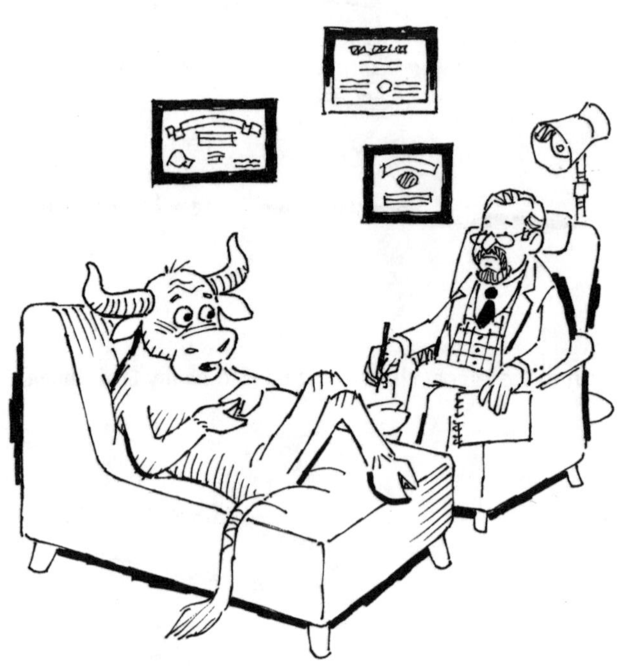

"I don't seem to be able to buck them off anymore."

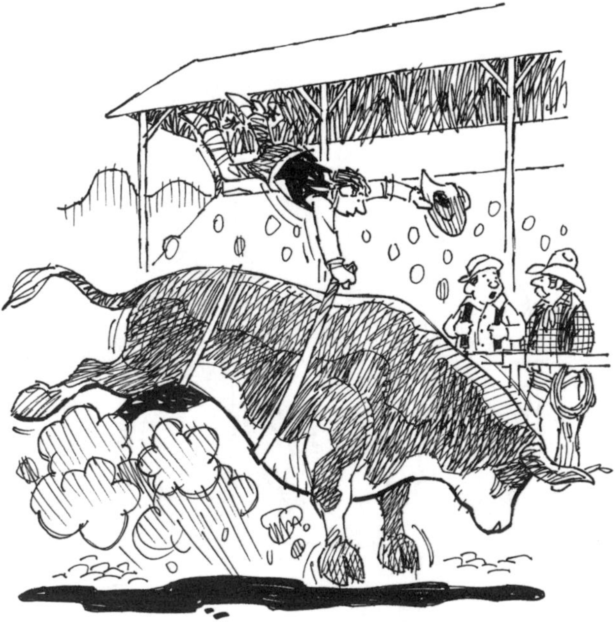

"It don't seem like an even match."

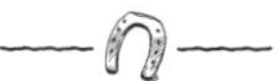

Country Squire was a world champion barrel racing horse.

He could beat a barrel every time.

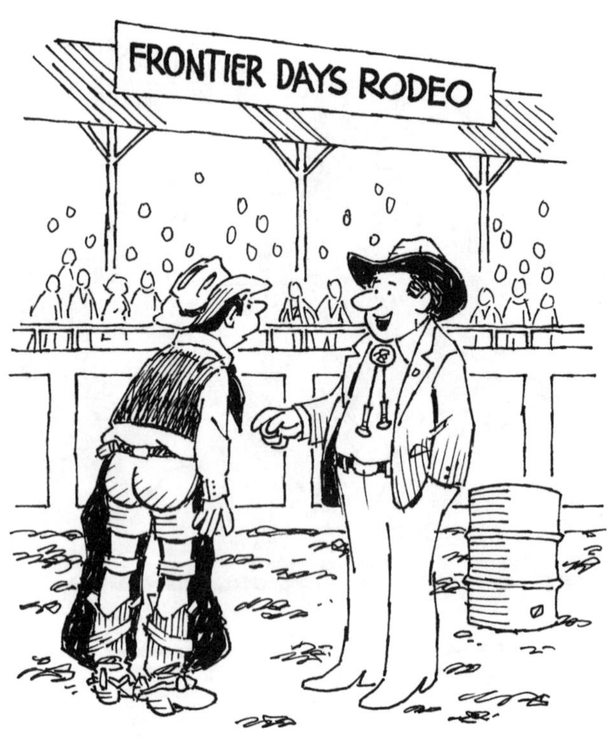

"Yer s'posed to wear jeans under them chaps, Albano."

The hard-bucking bull broke out of the chute and threw his rider in seconds. A rodeo clown quickly drew the bull's attention and led him across the rodeo arena. At the last moment, the clown sidestepped, and the bull crashed head-on into the solid wall beneath the bleachers, causing him to see stars. The crowd stood up and sang **The Star-Spangled Brahma.**

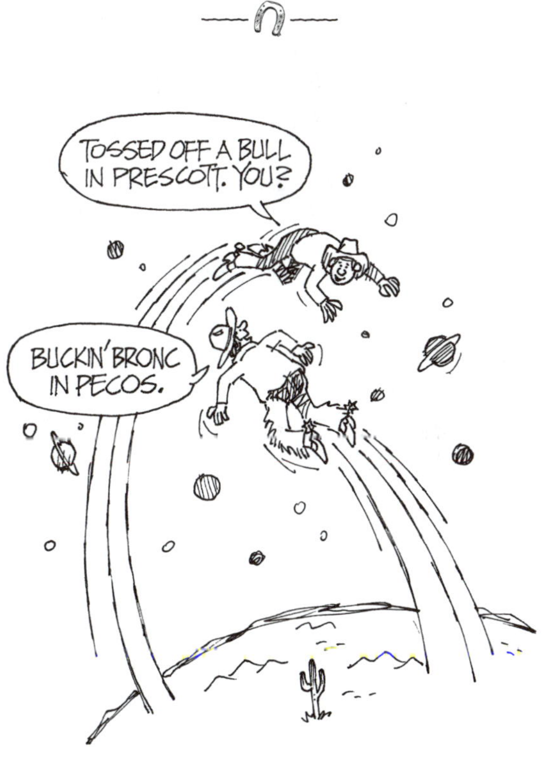

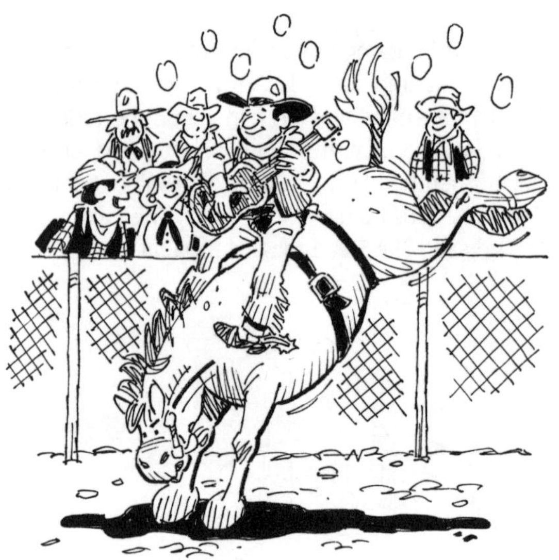

"This will be a hard act to follow!"

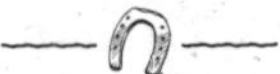

A cowboy who walks away from a rodeo without limping **didn't participate in it.**

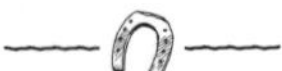

The rodeo announcer spoke into his mike, "Big Thunder is the fiercest of bucking broncs. **His latest rider was last seen over Seligman, Arizona."**

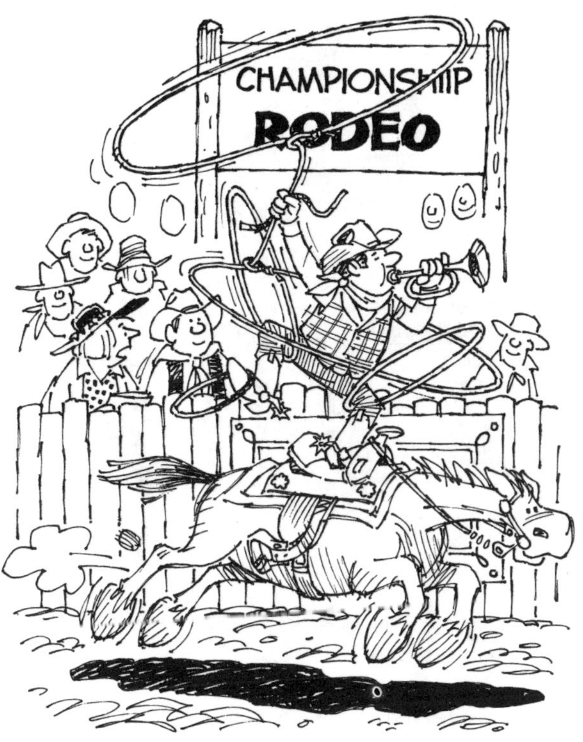

"What else can he do?"

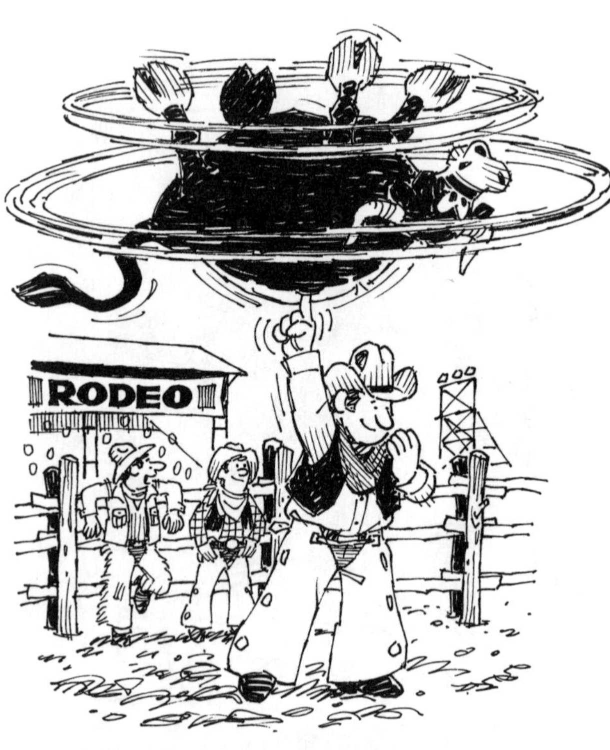

"Hazelton lends a new dimension to bull fighting."

A real rodeo cowboy doesn't mind breaking an arm . . .

. . . But getting thrown off into a cow pie hurts his feelings some.

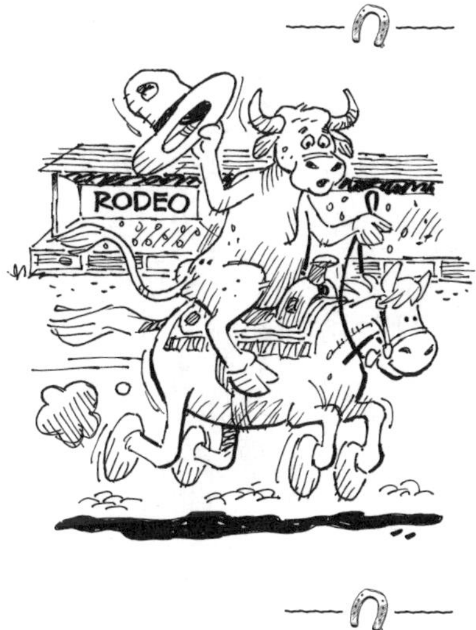

Bull riding is an event other than **a bull riding a horse.**

This dude's mistake was **waving a red flag at a stampeding bull,** thinking that would make him stop.

All that bouncing around on top of a bucking bronc could shake a cowboy's wallet loose – **which wouldn't make the cowboy much lighter!**

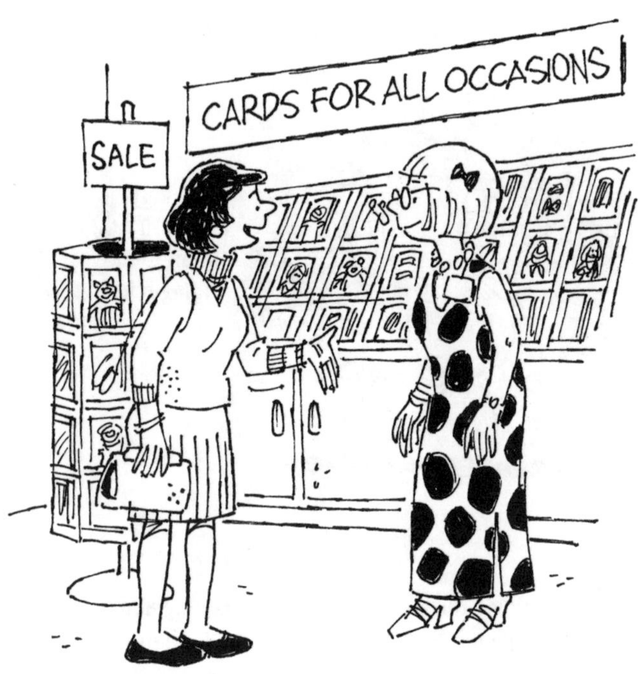

"Do you have something for a bull rider who swallowed his dentures?"

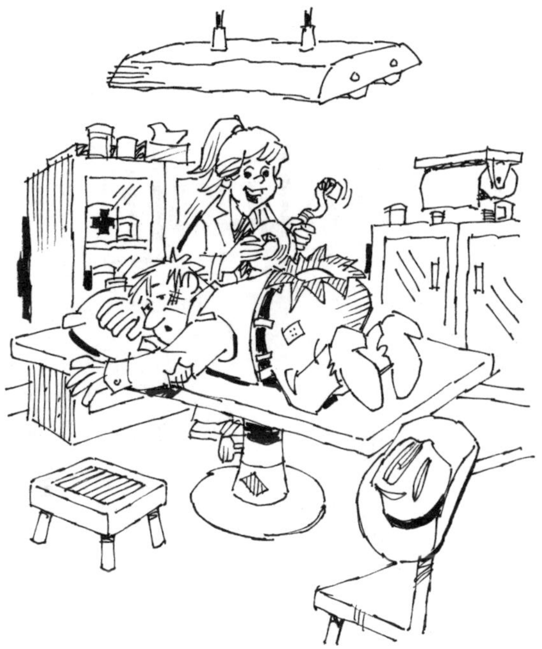

"Otherwise, how was the bull ride?"

The Swinging Doors

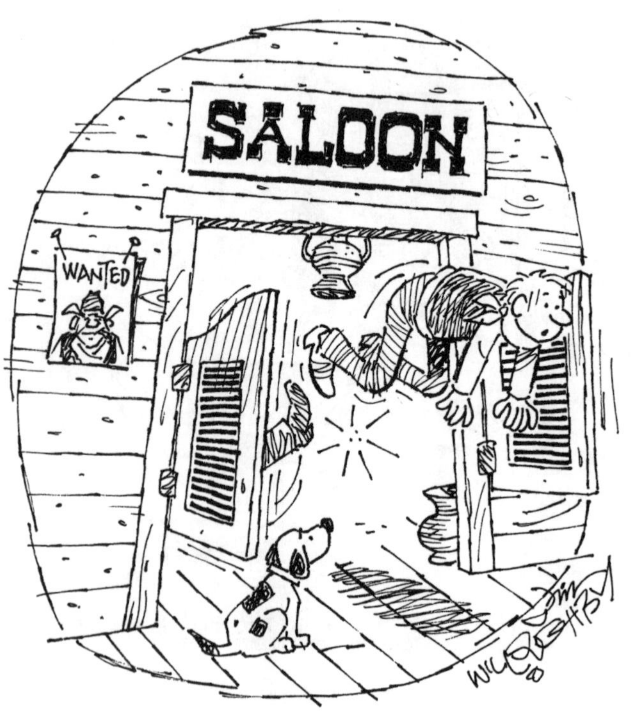

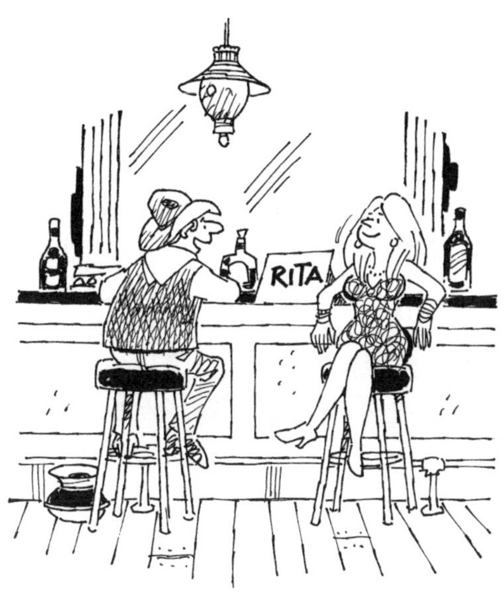

"You come here often?"

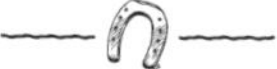

Hearing an old miner had been robbed and shot, a well-armed posse rode hell-bent for leather to his cabin. Leaning against the cabin's door jamb was Sourdough Slim, his rifle resting across his bony lap and a dozen bullet holes air-conditioning his shirt.

Hastily dismounting, the sheriff dashed up to Slim and spoke, **"We heard you was in trouble, Slim, and we come runnin' soon as the card game was over."**

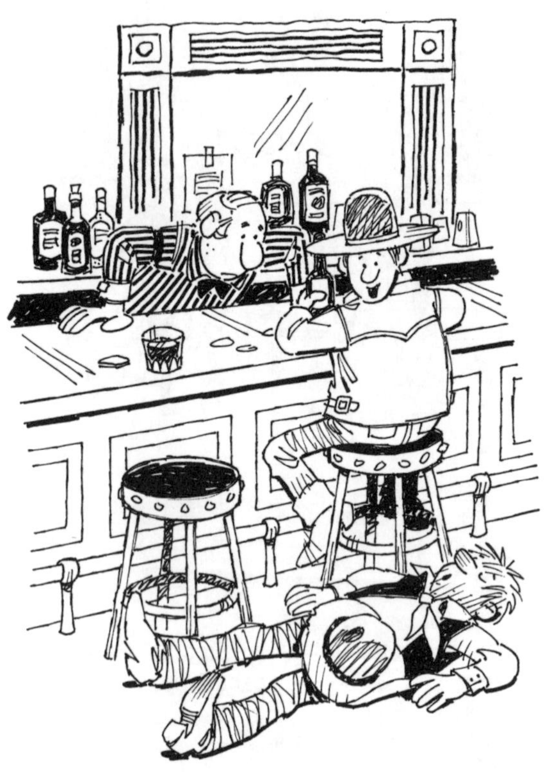

"He sits a horse better than a bar stool."

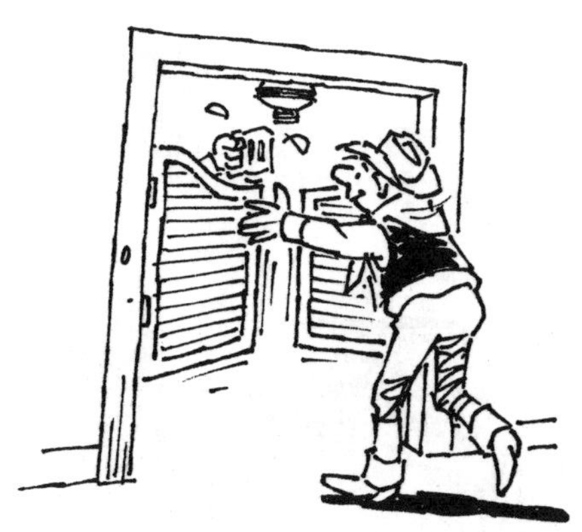

The doors swing in...

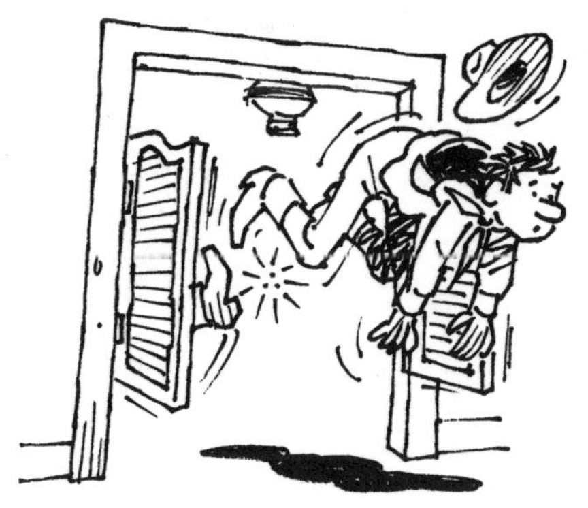

...and the doors swing out!

It's what saloons are all about...

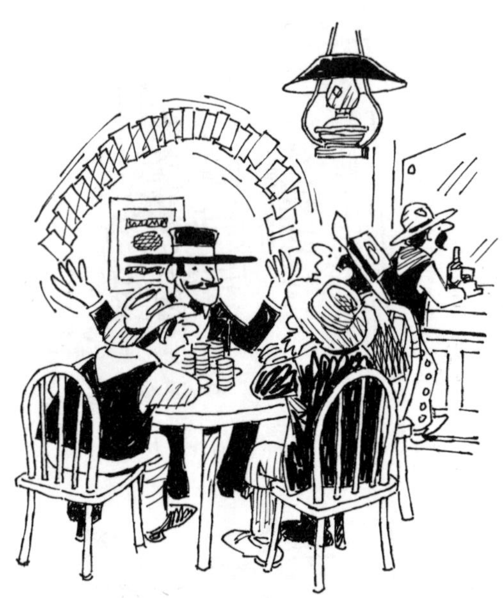

"Keep your eye on this guy!"

Billy the Kid was a nasty gunslinger, **not a young goat.**

Asked about his saloon's new revolving door, the owner responded, "It's great! **My inebriated patrons stagger out on one side and right back in on the other."**

A tough-looking gentleman walked into the town tavern and sat at the bar. When the barkeep inquired about the hanging rope suspended from the man's neck, he explained, **"I was putting up a clothesline and the rope got twisted around my neck."**

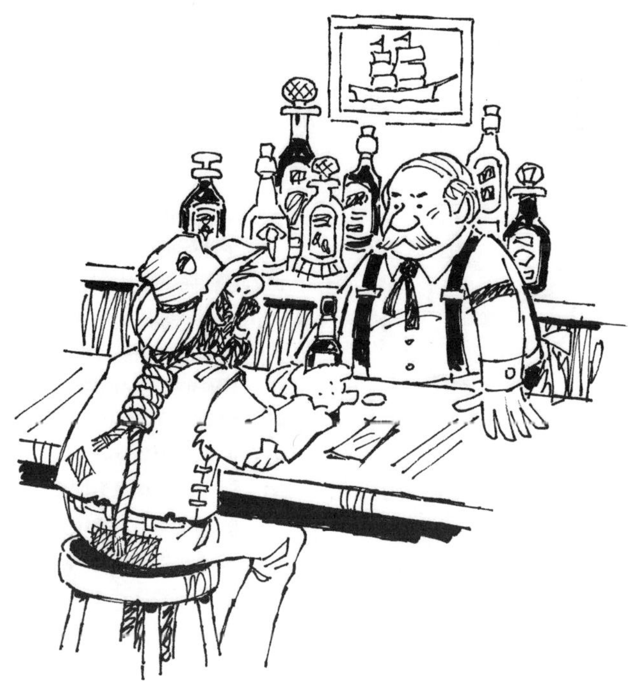

A tired cowboy left the saloon and found that his horse had been stolen from the hitching post. He went back into the saloon, flipped his gun in the air, caught it above his head, and fired a shot into the ceiling.

"Which one of you sidewinders stole my horse?" he yelled.

No one answered.

"All right," he said, "I'm going to have another beer, and if my horse ain't back outside by the time I'm finished, I'm going to have to do what I done in Texas, and I don't like to do what I had to do in Texas."

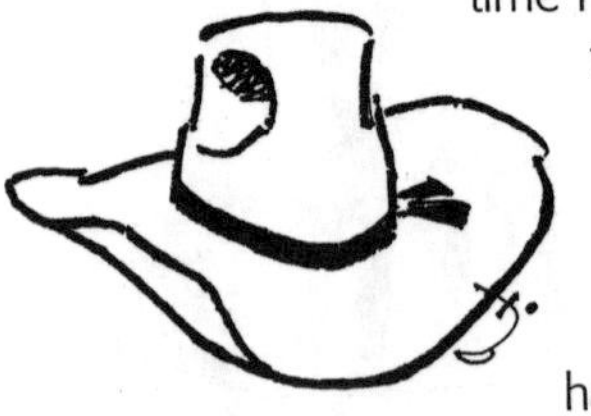

Some of the bar patrons shifted nervously. The cowboy had his beer, walked outside, and found his horse tied to the post.

He mounted up and started to ride out of town. The barkeep wandered out and asked, "Say, pardner, what DID happen in Texas?"

The stranger turned to him and replied, **"I had to walk home."**

(This yarn's from an anonymous source.)

In a back corner of the Turkey Gulch Saloon, a card game was going full swing. Suddenly, the floor opened beneath one player, and he disappeared, chair and all, into the basement. There was no change of expression on the face of another player as he looked down and commented, **"Looks like Gerba is dropping out."**

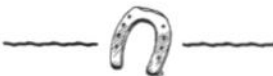

There ain't nuthin' like a pair of .45s **to put a dude in a dancin' mood.**

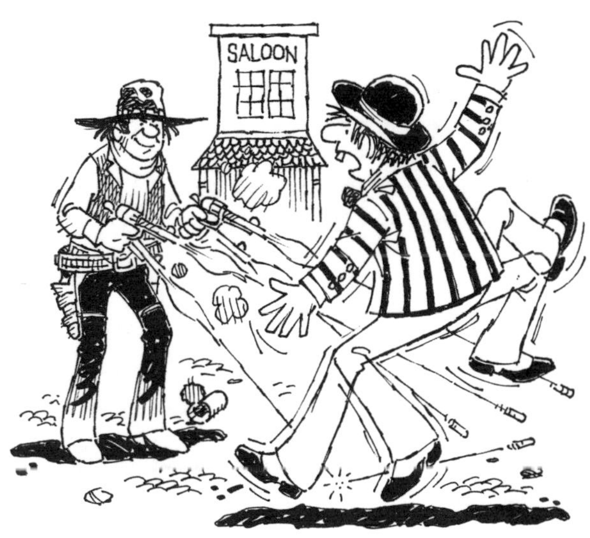

Two cowhands were on the floor of the Old Palace Saloon pounding the daylights out of each other. "How did it start?" a buckaroo at the bar inquired. Another replied, **"One called the other a sheepherder."**

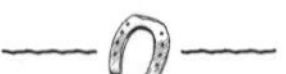

Calamity Jane was so ugly that **the barkeep would hand out dark glasses when she walked into a saloon.**

Big Nose Kate smelled so bad, **when she ate a clove of garlic, it was like a breath of fresh air.**

Stragnell the Strangler was so tough that when he ambled into a saloon, **the pool balls leaped into the pockets.**

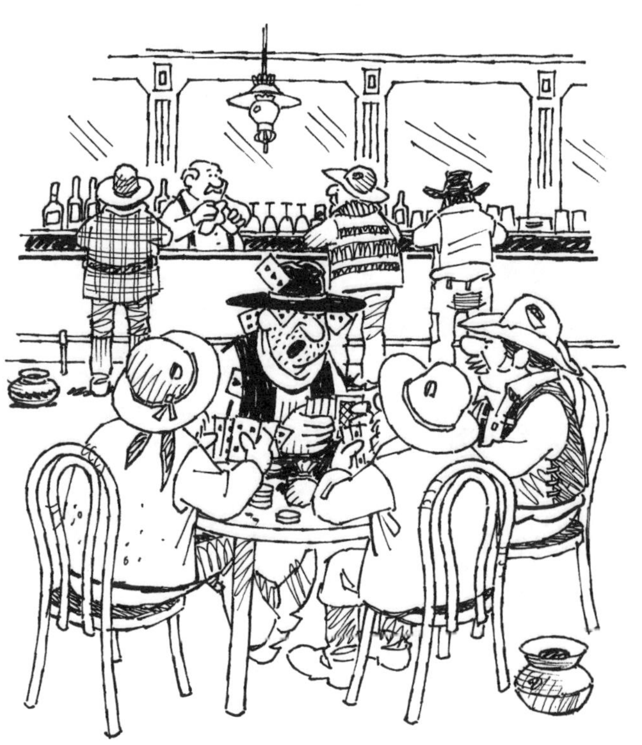

"Are you sayin' I'm cheating?"

"Hi, Doc, How am I?"

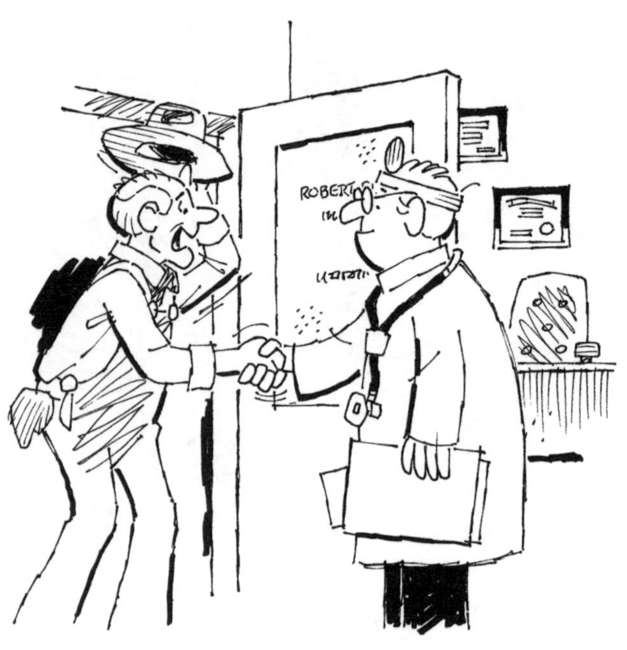

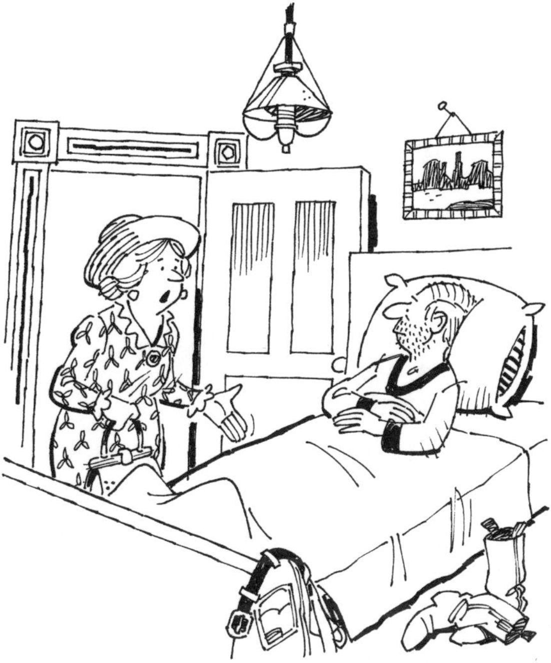

"I've been out checking on funeral prices. You can't afford to die, Paw."

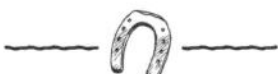

Luther felt really sick, too sick to ride the 7 miles into town. He rang up the doctor and asked, "Hey, Doc, do you make house calls?"

The doctor responded, "Where does your house hurt?"

"How long have you been troubled with these symptoms of nausea and stress?" the doctor asked Wiley Willie.

Willie moaned, "Since I got your last bill."

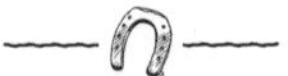

"Just fill out these papers and the doctor will be right with you," the nurse told Tenderloin, handing him a large stack of forms.

"Hell," the ailing Tenderloin came back, "I'll be dead before I can fill all these out!"

"In that event," the nurse said, "we'll make a proper notation in your records."

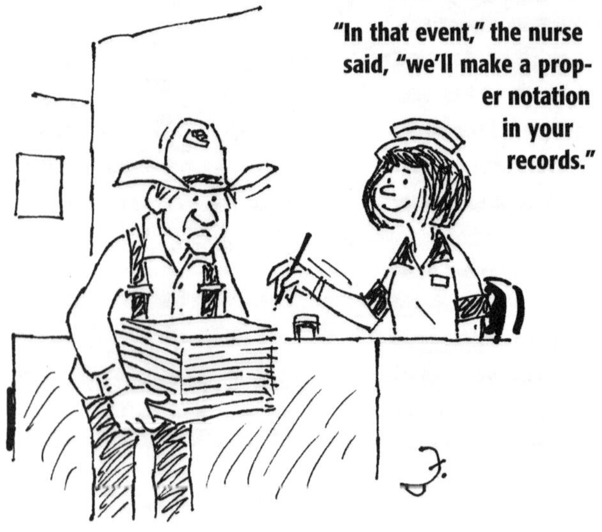

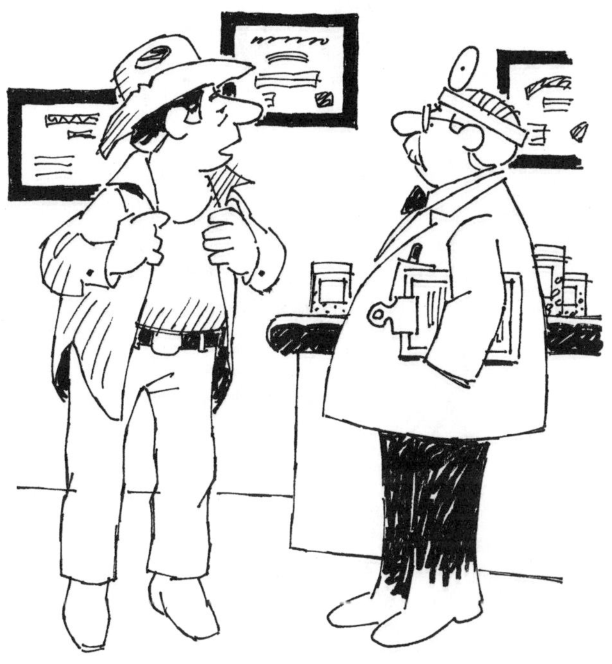

"One thing, Doc — no discouraging words!"

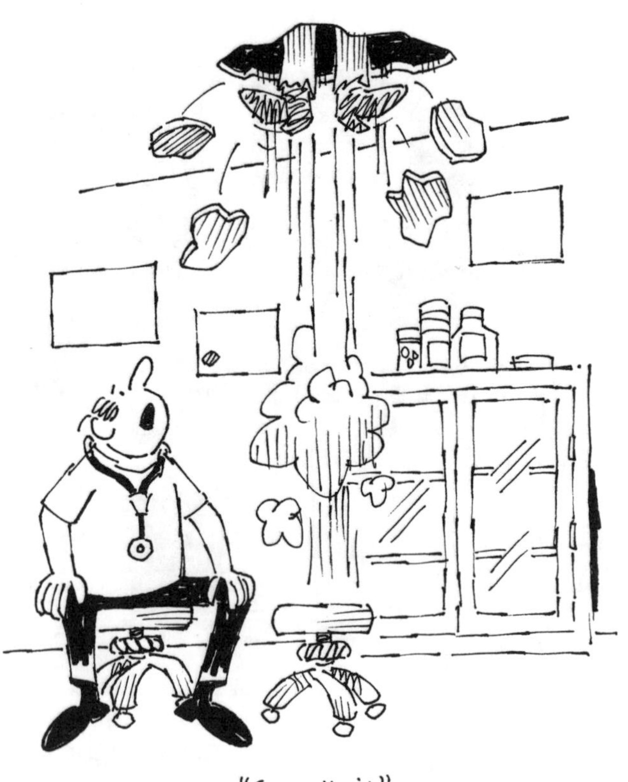

"Gesundheit."

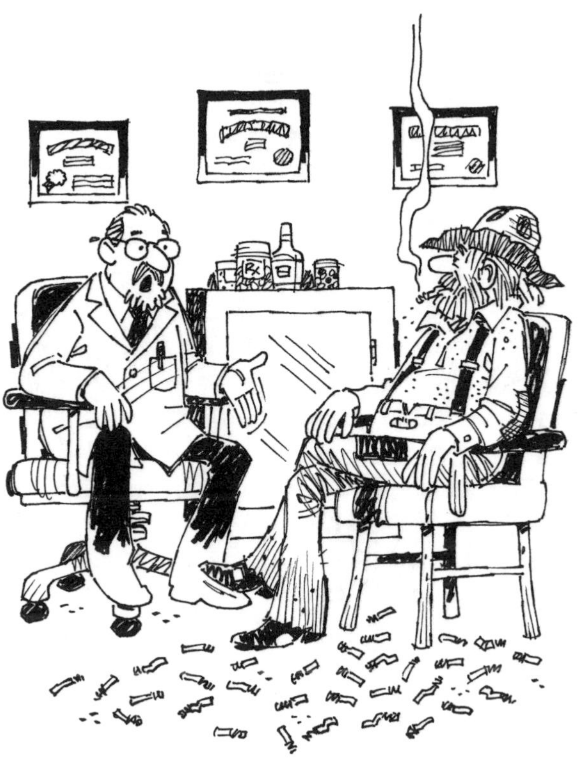

"Another thing, Duke, I'd give up the smoking."

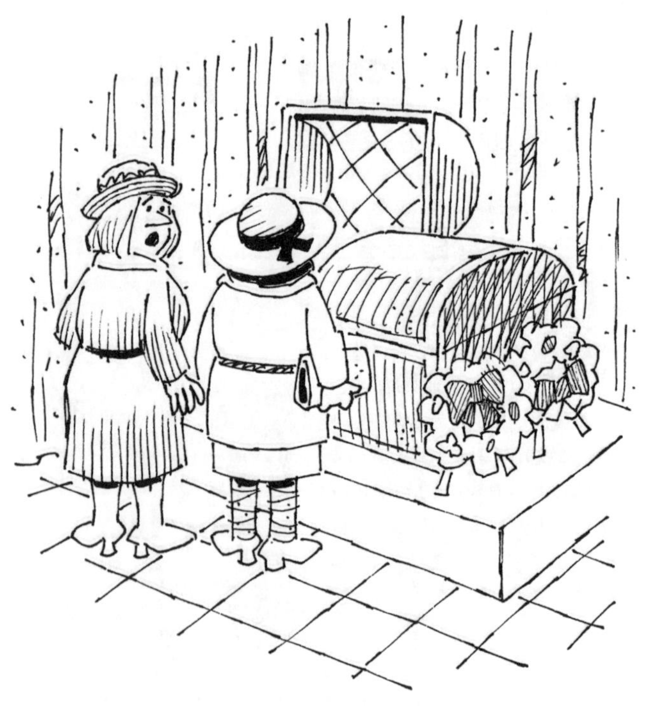

"I kept nagging him to go see a doctor. Then, one day, he did."

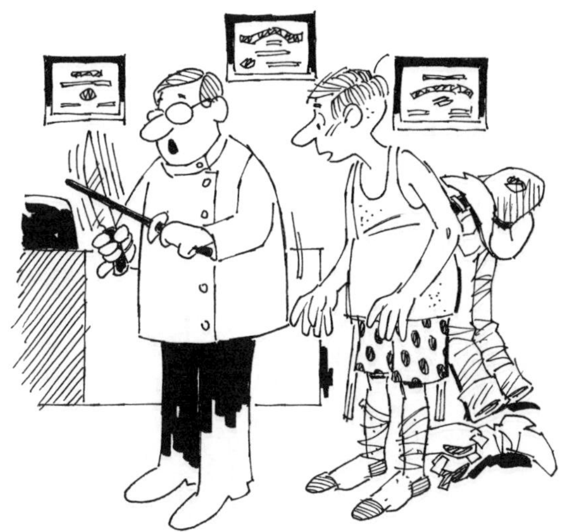

"I'm afraid we'll have to operate, Nelson."

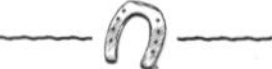

"When was the last time you saw a doctor?" the registration nurse asked Fiddlin' Phil.

"The day I was born," Phil said.

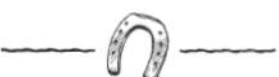

Clem told the doctor, "My heart keeps going clippity clop." To that, the doctor replied, **"Try getting a job where you don't have to ride a horse."**

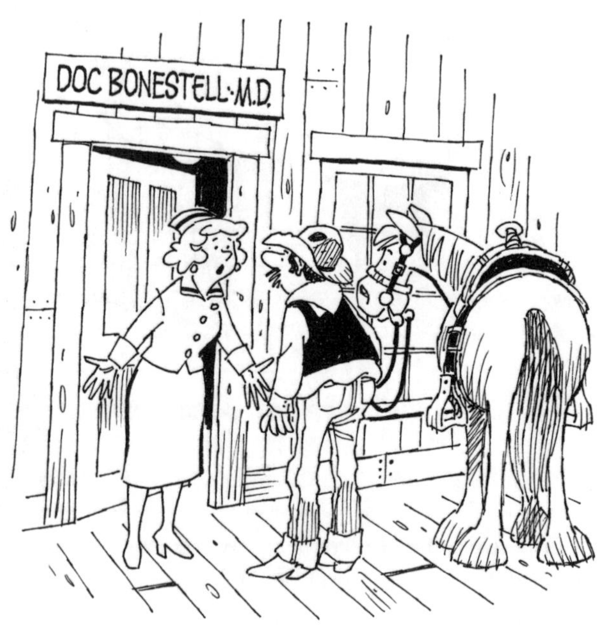

"I'm sorry, Mr. Rawhide. The doctor says your horse will have to wait outside."

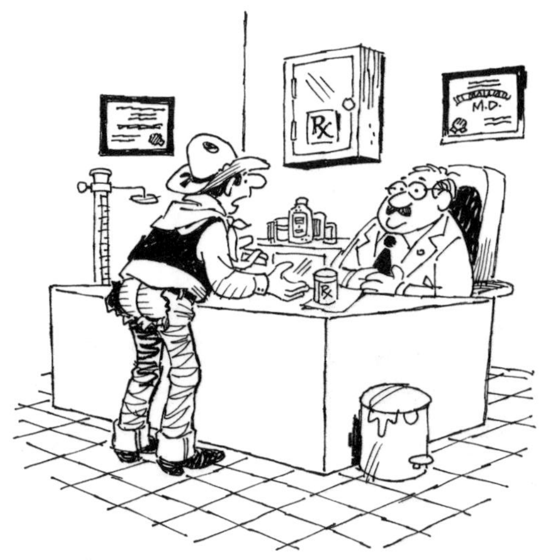

"My job requires that I sit a lot."

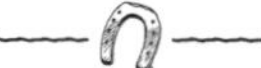

Clancy, on arriving back at his shack, told his little woman about his visit to the hospital in town. "I was sedated, inoculated, fixated, barbituated, radiated, and medicated," he said disgustedly.

"Sounds like you were ultraviolated," she responded.

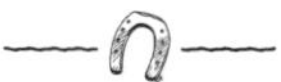

By the time you're put in one, **you don't care whether it's a pine box or some other kind of wood.**

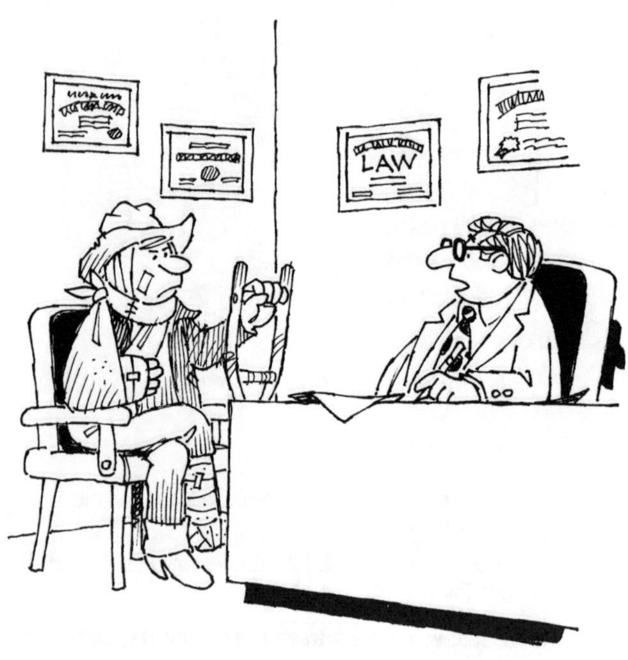

"To my knowledge, Mr. Crowley, nobody has ever sued a horse before."

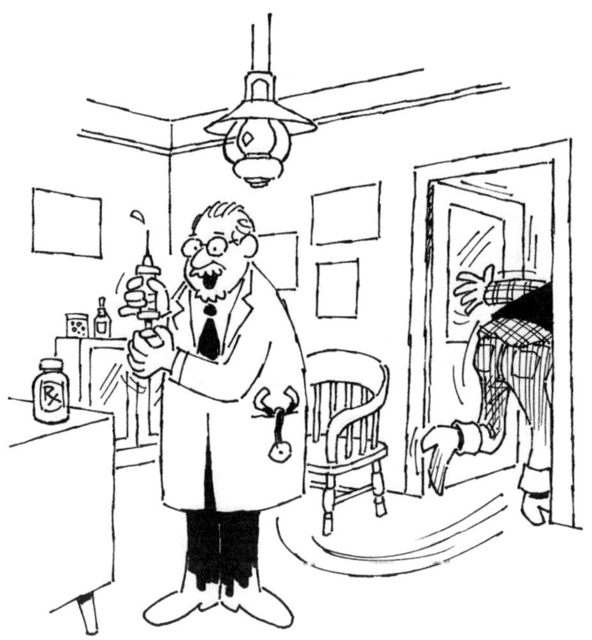

"This should get you up and going, Elwood!"

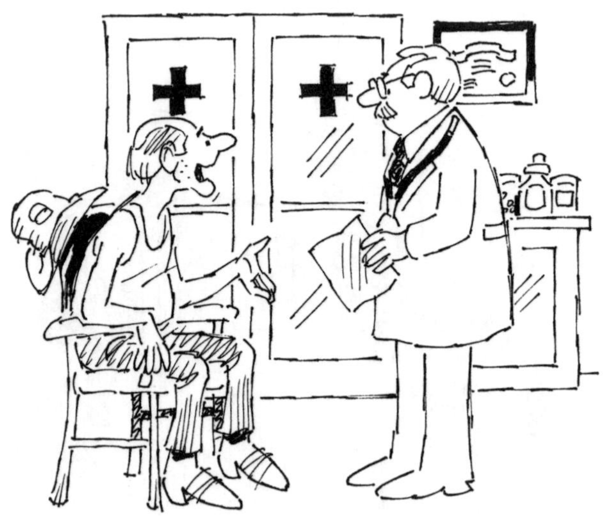

"You've given me pills for arthritis, pleurisy, back pains, stomach ache, to settle my nerves, and to help me sleep. Have you got any that would make my teeth grow back in?"

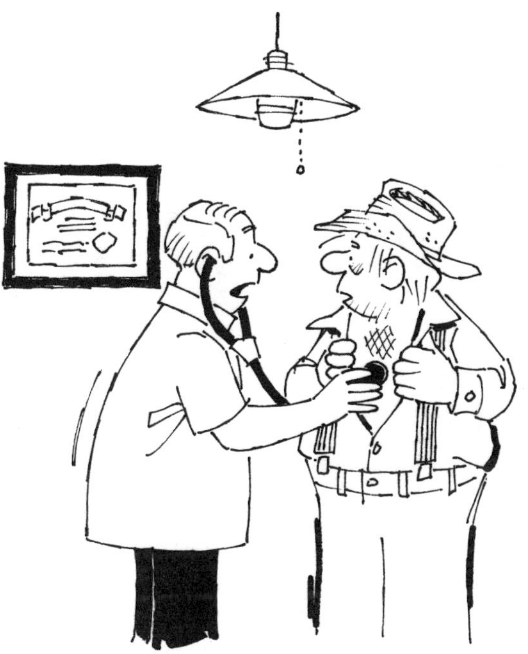

"It sounds like a thundering herd."

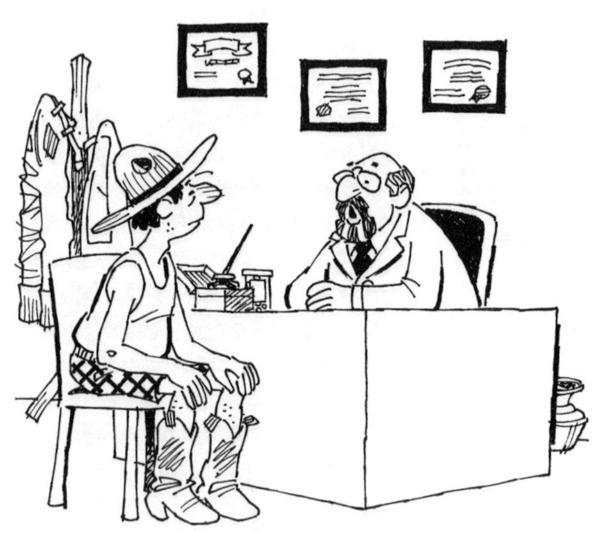

"If you were a horse, Rimshot, they would put you out to pasture."

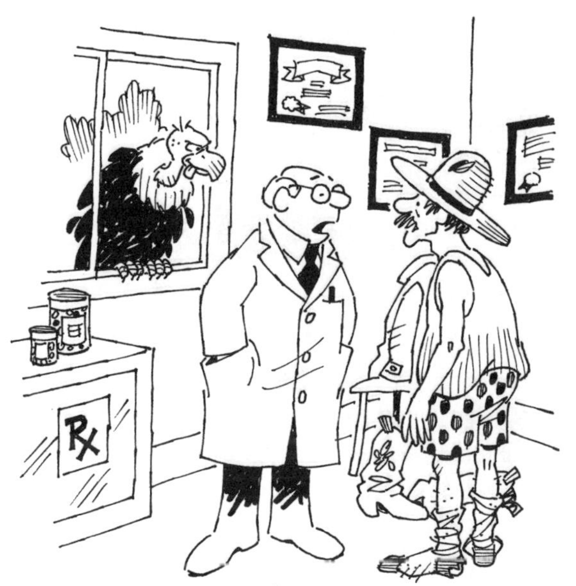

"I'm afraid it doesn't look good for you, Luther."

Sheep in the Meadow, Cows in the Corn

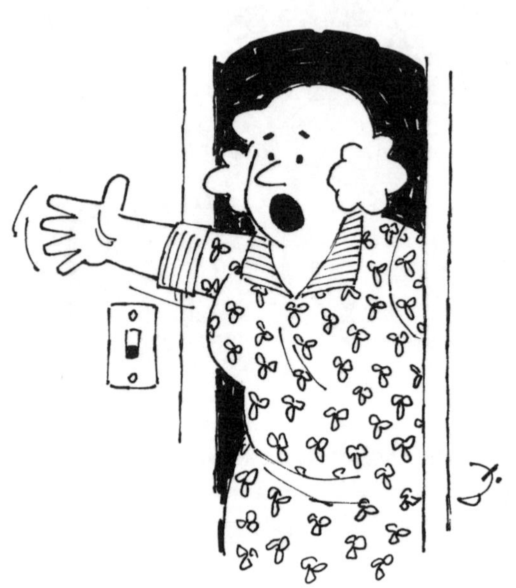

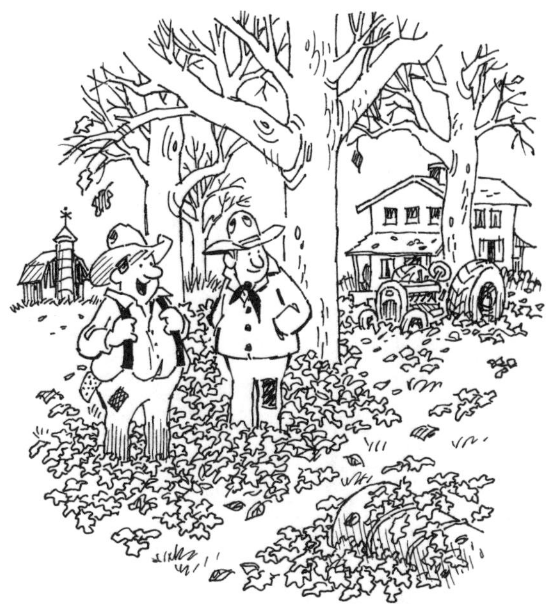

"We had a great crop of leaves this year."

There are some cowhands who figure a woman's place is in the home – **right after work.**

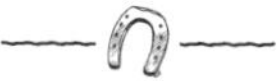

After his wife had passed away, old Jeb would have watched television – **except for the lack of one.**

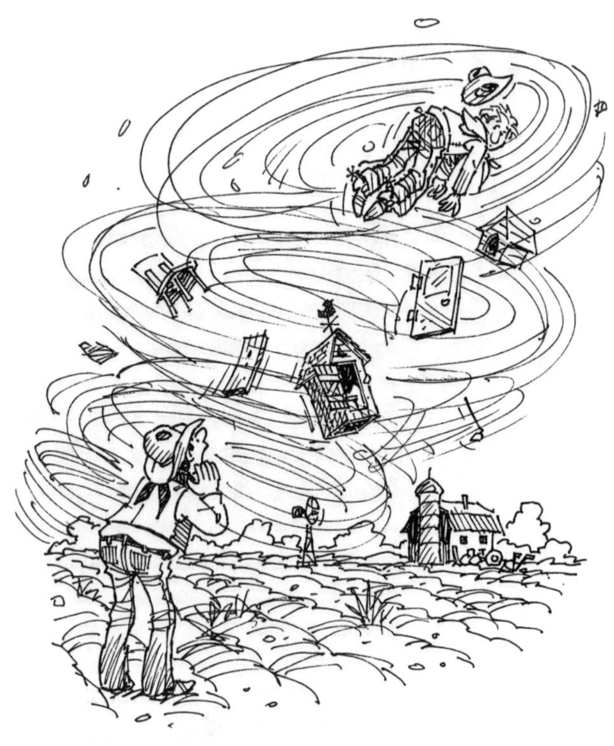

"Don't forget to write."

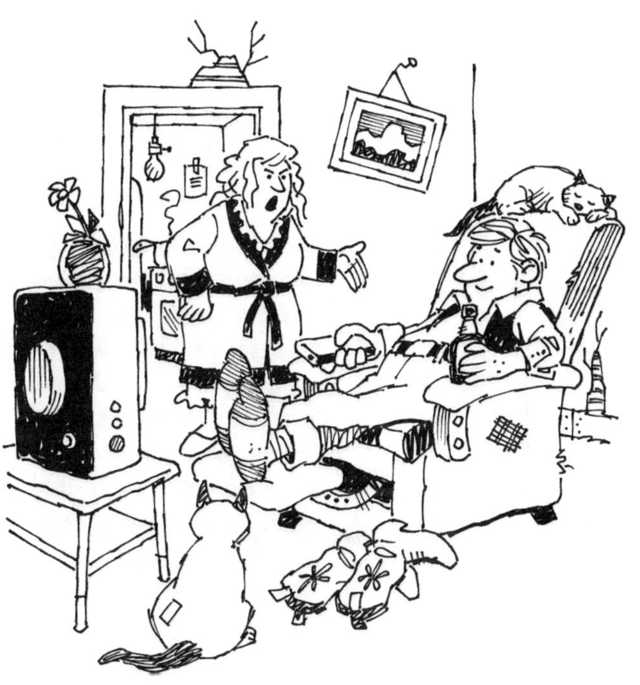

"I'll bet Gary Cooper didn't lie around drinking beer and watching football on his days off."

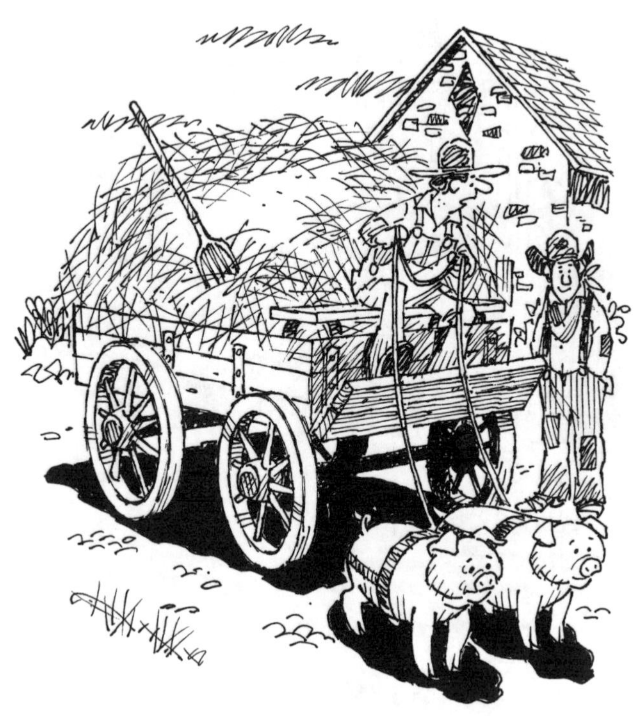

"My horses strayed off somewhere."

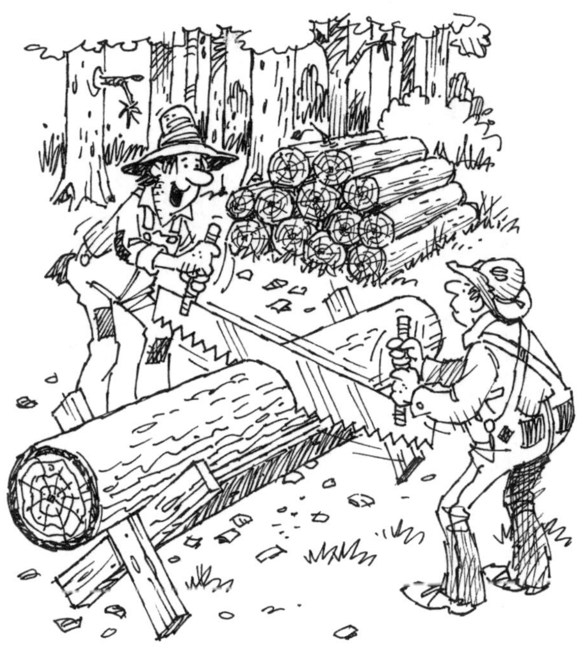

"Seesaw, Marjorie Daw..."

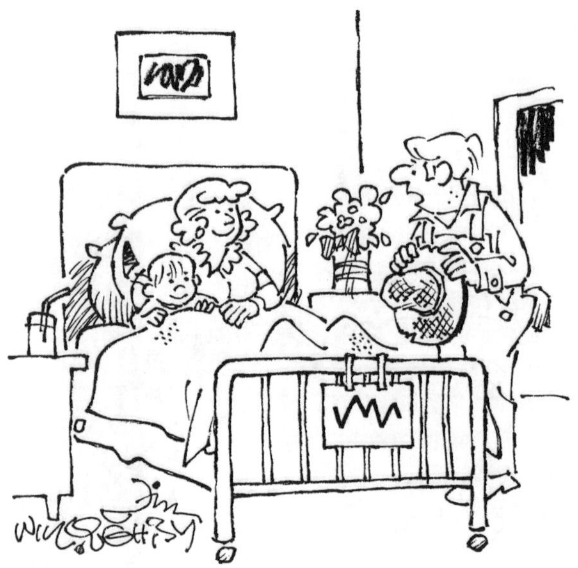

"How long 'til he can ride roundup?"

Elmer won his wife in one of those raffles. **It caused him to give up gambling.**

If your wife is all of a sudden more chipper, smiling and singing, **someone else may be doing your homework.**

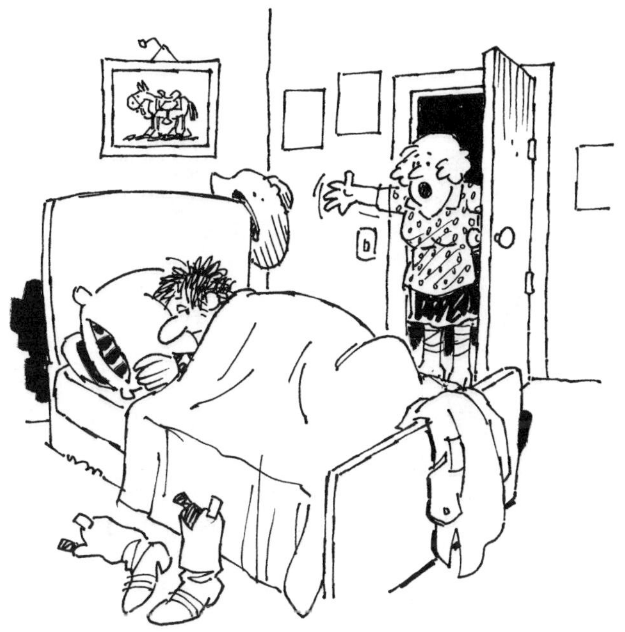

"Wake up, Wilborn! The sheep are in the meadow,
The cows are in the corn."

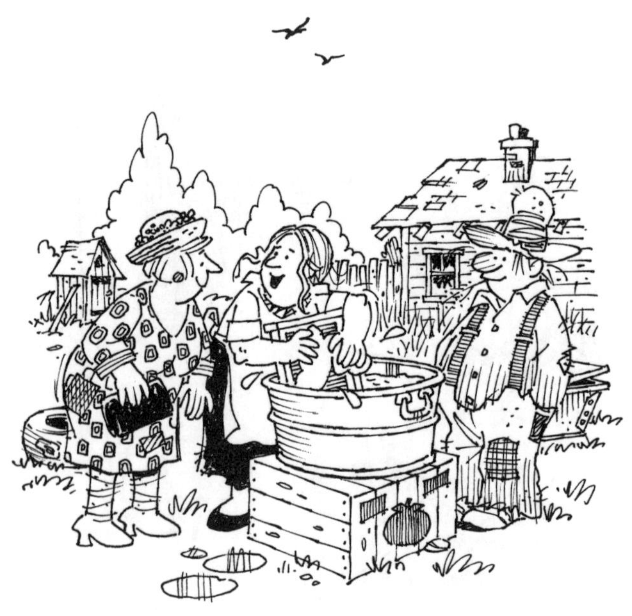

"Jude bought me this new washing machine."

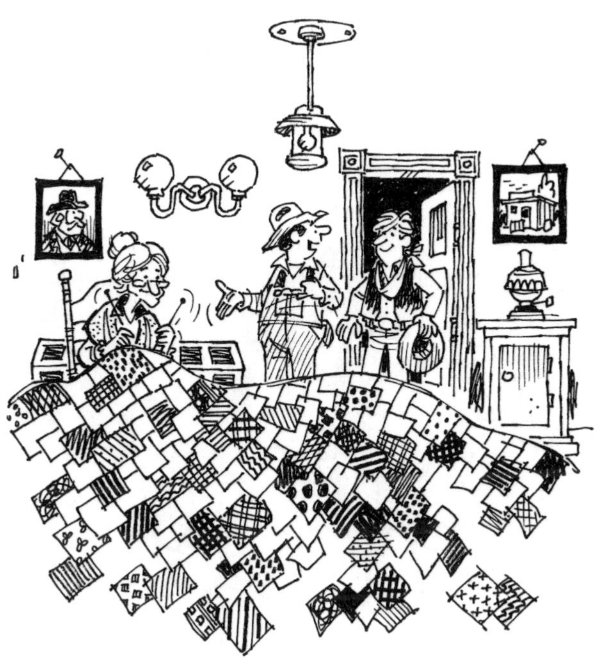

"She's been stichin' that quilt for 30 years. It's big enough to cover half of Arizona."

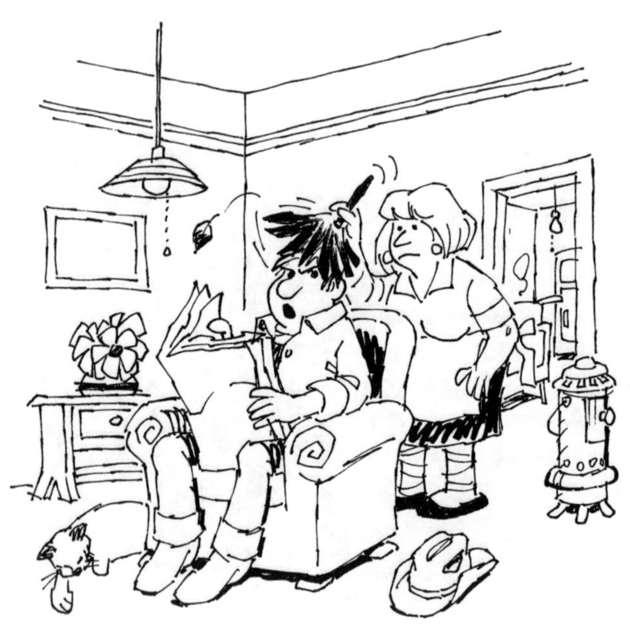

"Elizabeth, you treat me like just a piece of furniture!"

Jamboree ain't a bread spread . . .

. . . And Ma Kettle is not a Dutch Oven?

—∩—

If your girlfriend makes good cornbread, **marry her.**

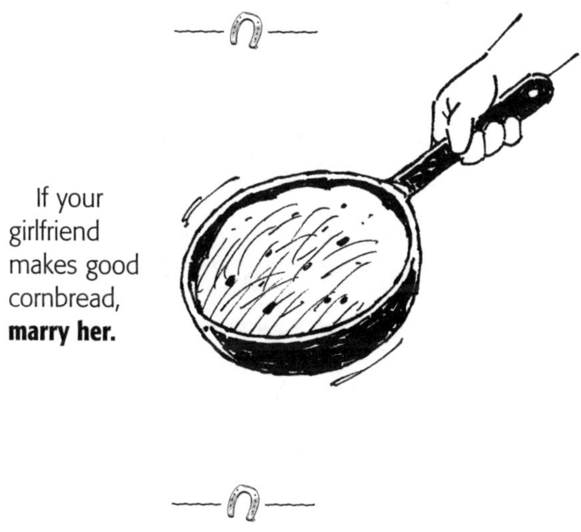

—∩—

Stagestop Stan says the only thing as gaping as the Grand Canyon is **his mother-in-law's mouth.**

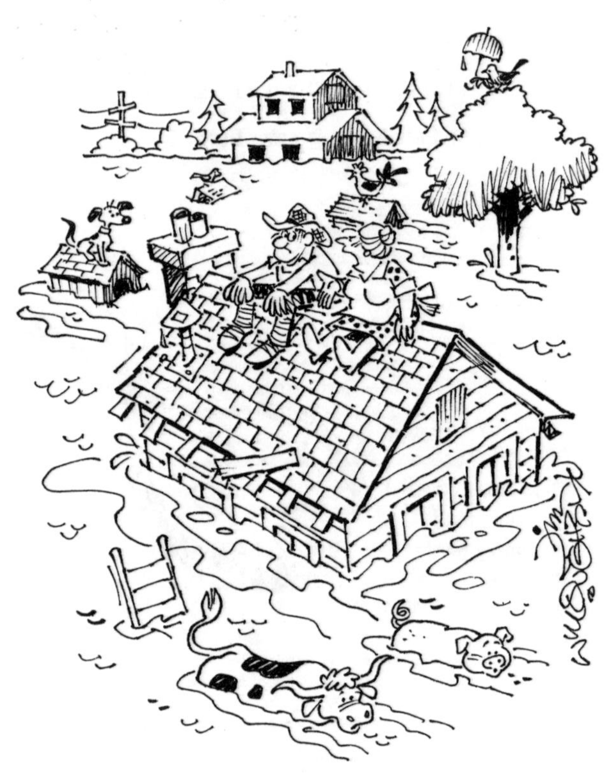

"I kept telling you,
'Fix that leaky faucet!'"

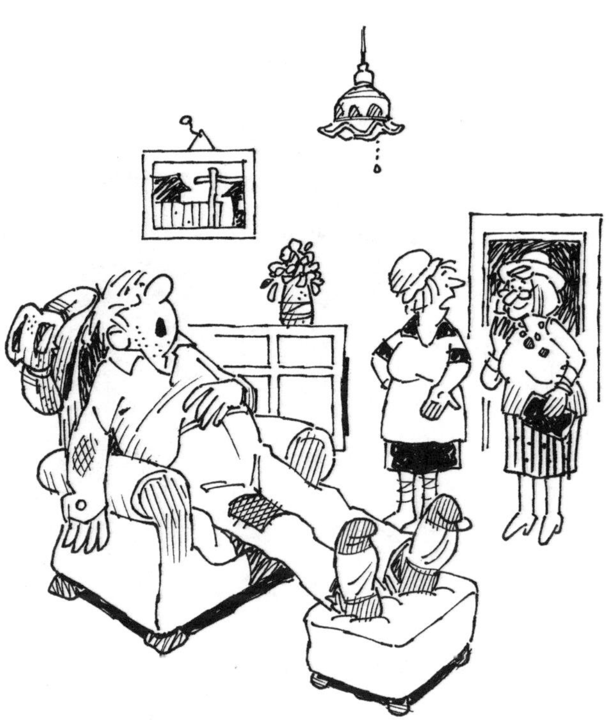

"Monty don't feel well today. That's been his story for 30 years."

Don't Become a Cowboy If...

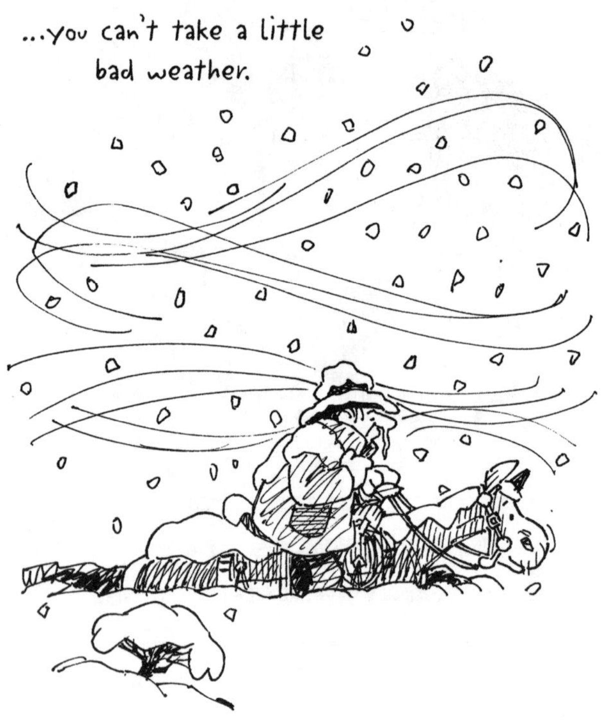

Don't become a cowboy if...

...you can't tell a bull from a heifer.

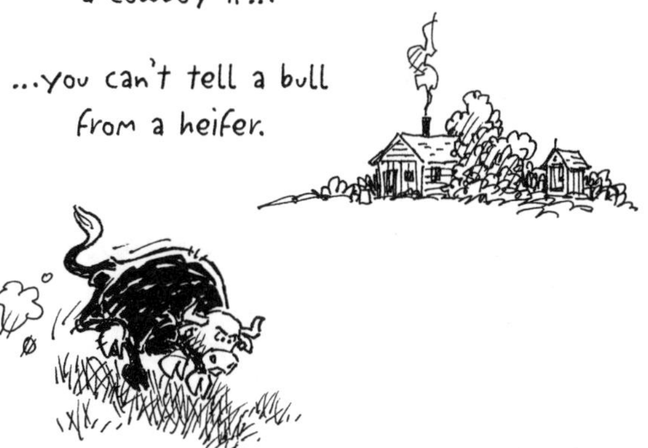

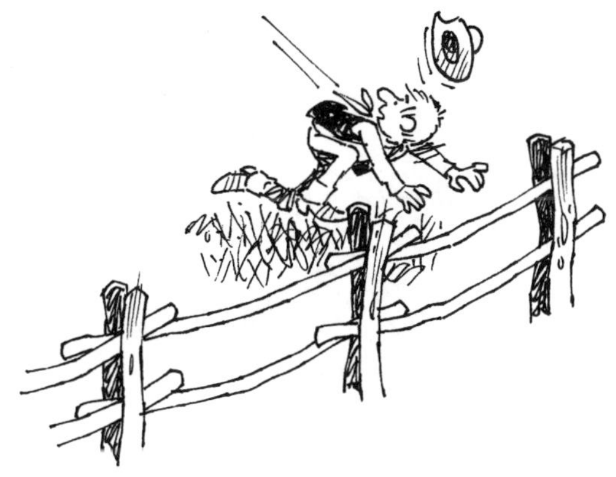

Don't become
a cowboy if...

...you don't like beans.

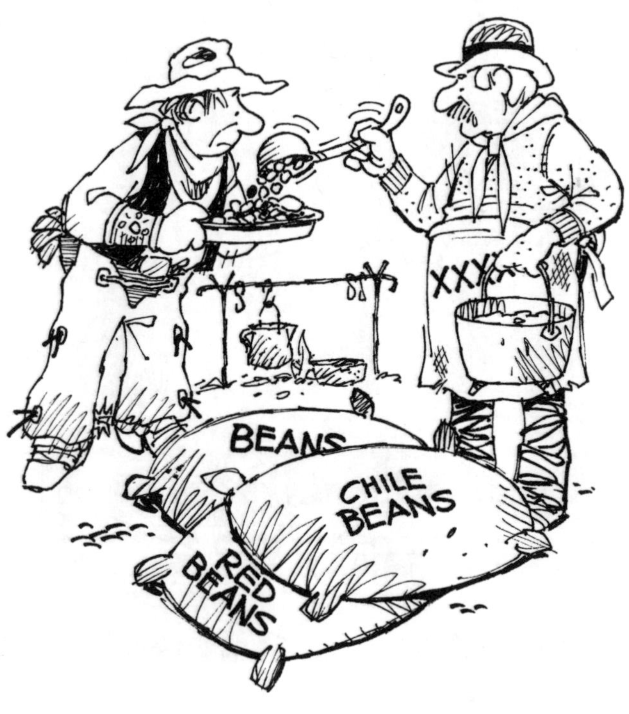

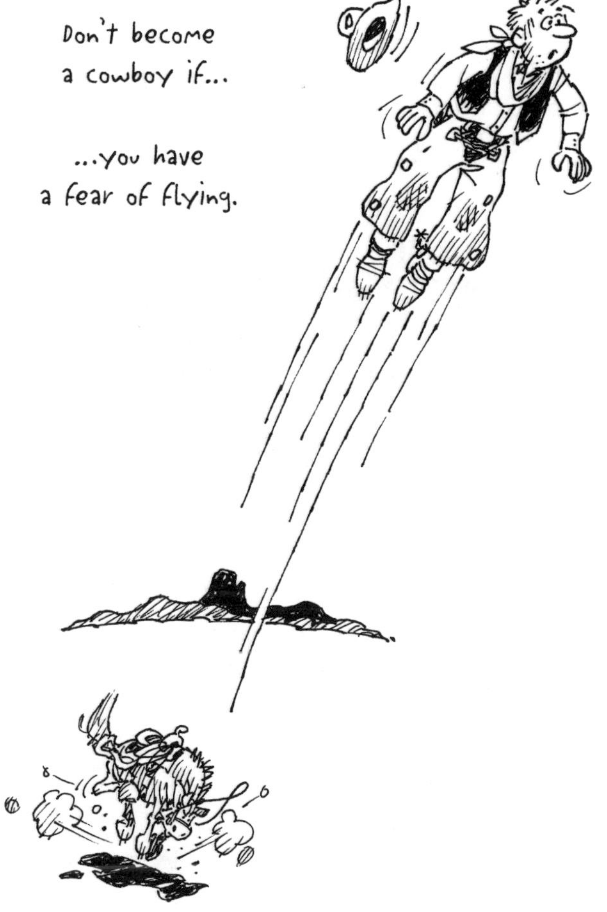
Don't become
a cowboy if...
...you have
a fear of flying.

Don't become
a cowboy if...

...you can't shoe
a horse properly.

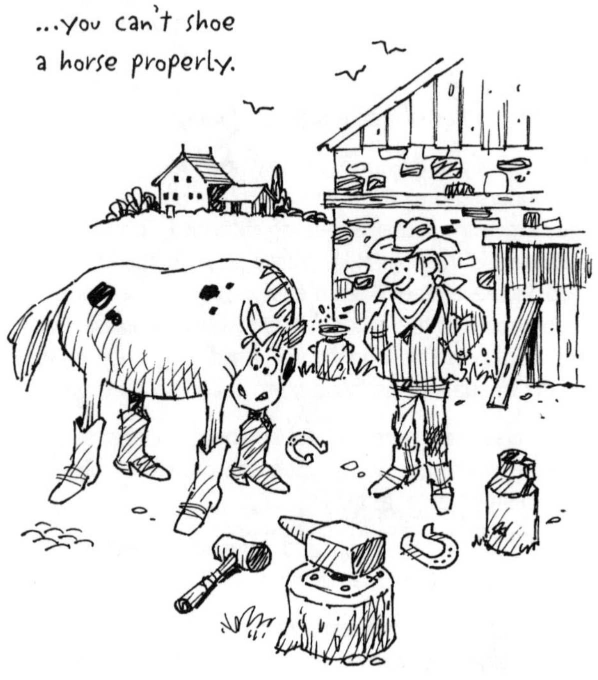

Don't become
a cowboy if...

...you can't pick yourself up,
dust yourself off, and
start all over again.

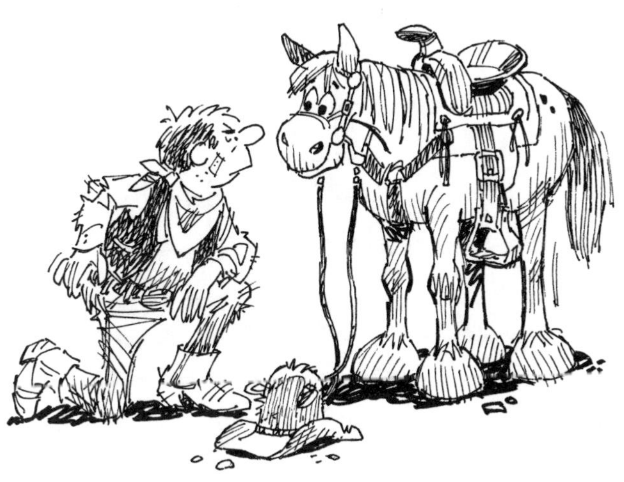

View from the Pew

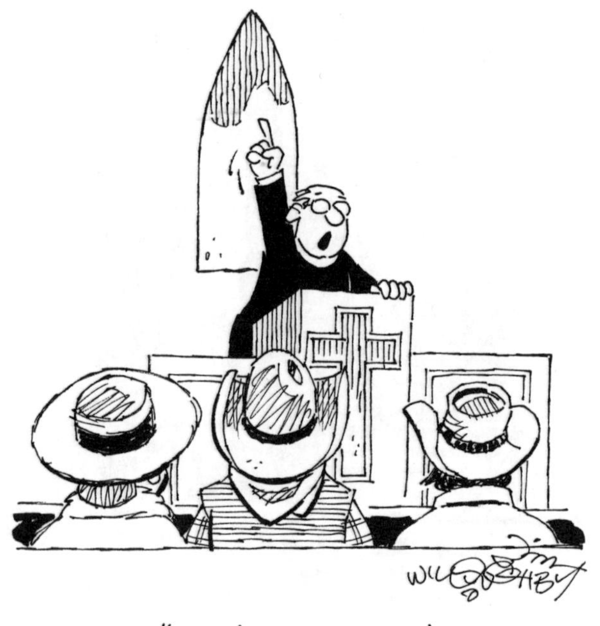

"We will all meet again
at that great cow pasture in the sky."

Two haloed angels observed another with three halos. One commented, **"I can't stand his haloer-than-thou attitude."**

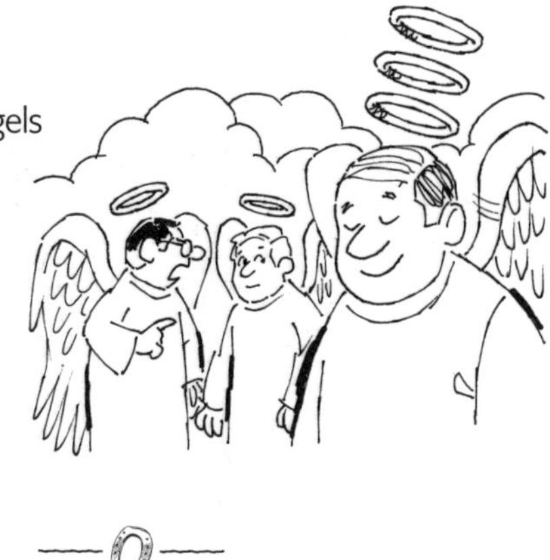

You can't find fault with the doings of someone who **doesn't do anything.**

In a little rural church along the Colorado River, they baptize by total immersion. **Scuba equipment is optional.**

You always get a warm feeling in church, **especially over near the heater.**

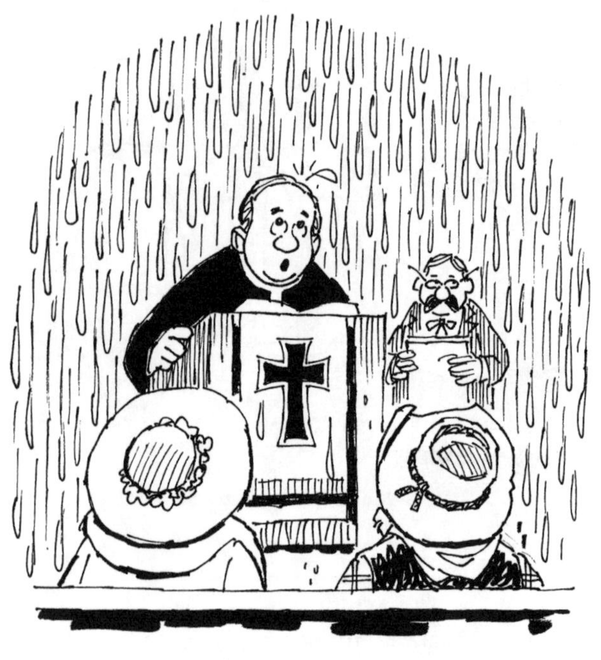

"...and now, a report from our roofing committee..."

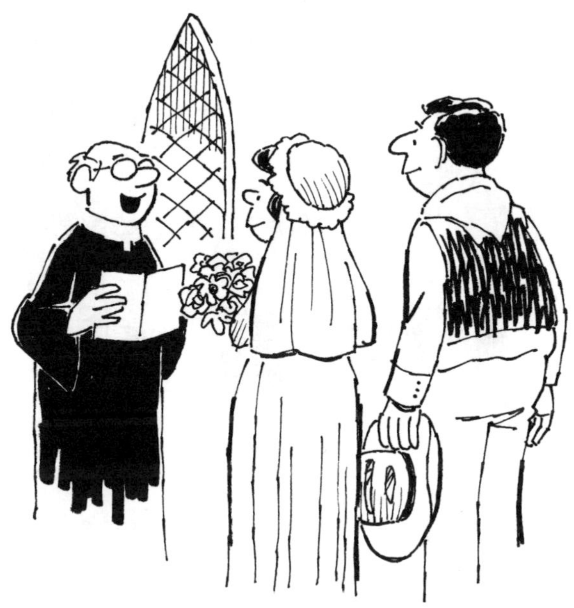

"...and do you, Ralph, take this woman to be hitched to for the rest of your life?"

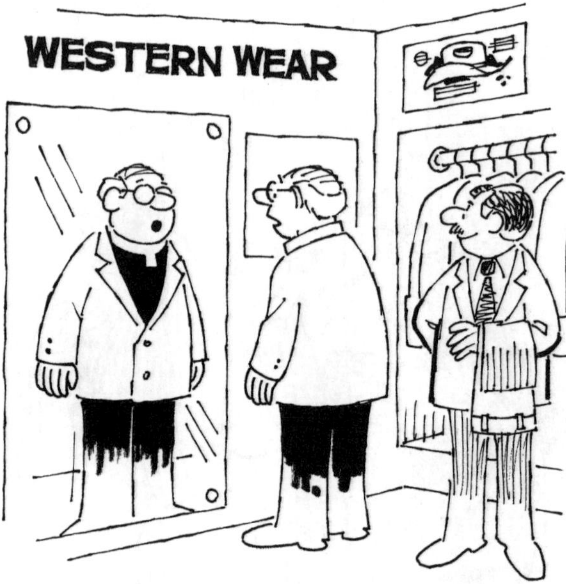

WESTERN WEAR

"Do you have something a little racier?"

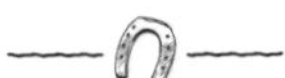

A bachelor cowboy was thoroughly impressed with a comely lass at a church social and finally summoned the nerve to approach her. He told her he thought she was an angel.

"Not yet," she countered demurely.

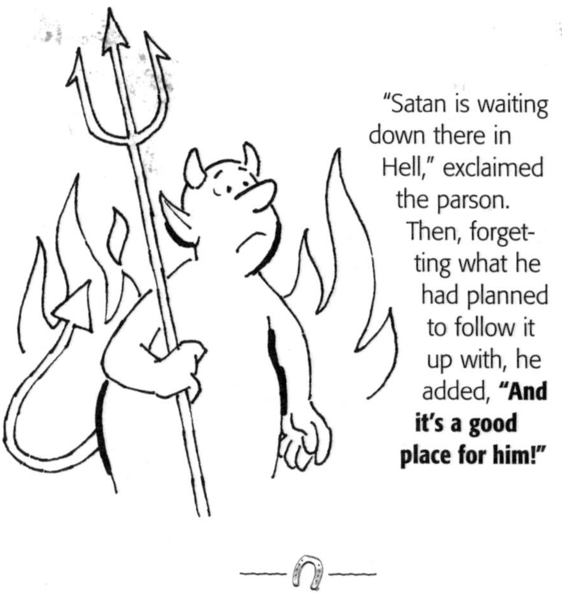

"Satan is waiting down there in Hell," exclaimed the parson. Then, forgetting what he had planned to follow it up with, he added, **"And it's a good place for him!"**

The nice thing about dying is **you only need to do it once.**

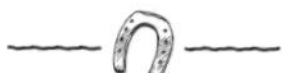

A ranch foreman entered the church and was greeted by one of the deacons, who asked if there was any place special he'd like to sit. **"In first class, of course," replied the foreman.**

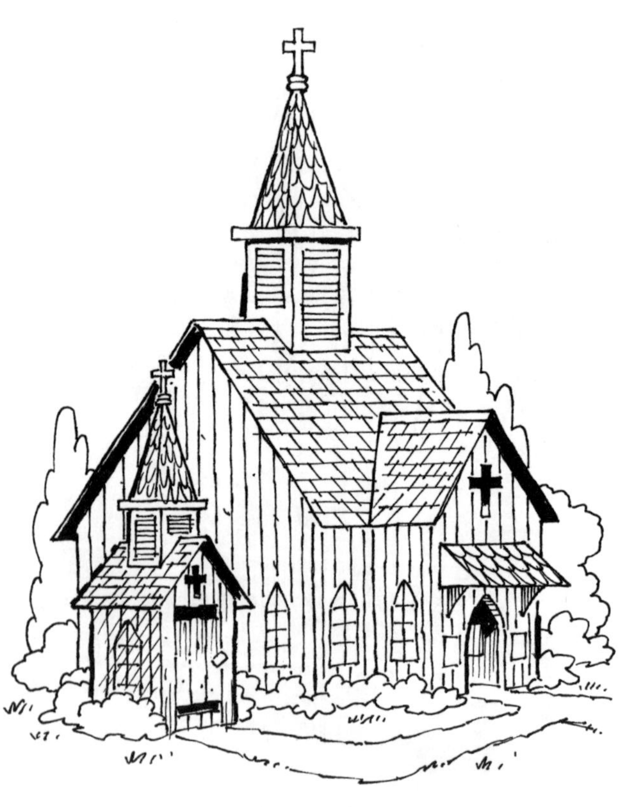

Mrs. Murphy regretted talking her attorney husband into attending services with her when, part way through the sermon, he leaped to his feet and, waving a finger in the air, addressed the parson, **"Objection! Calls for conjecture."**

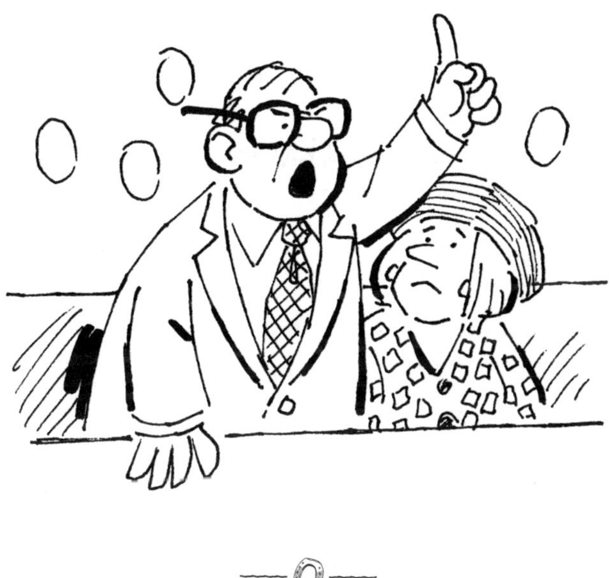

When his wife asked him if the deceased Mr. Brown was going to be buried or cremated, the cowboy answered, **"I don't know. He isn't returning calls."**

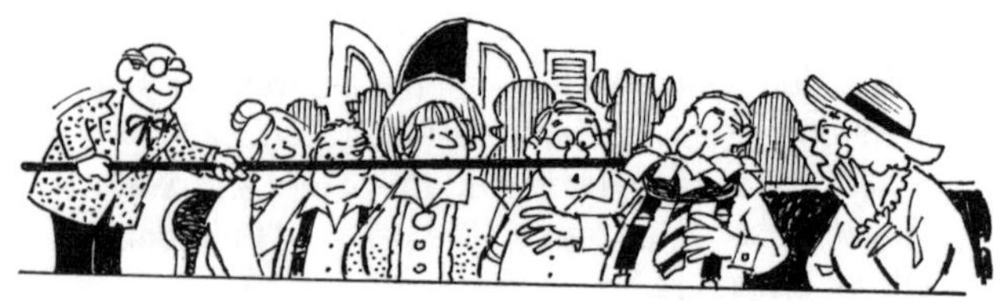

"Oh, Walt, put something in."

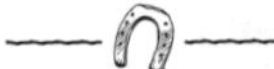

Be careful when you pick up a sealed vase. **It might contain an ancestor.**

Following an impressive rehearsal of 'Rock of Ages', the choir leader said, "Very good, gang. Let's do it one more time, though, **and this time let's leave out the doo-dabba-do bit."**

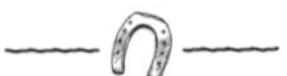

Many in last Sunday's congregation were spellbound by Reverend Van Riper's sermon. **A nearby passing freight train broke the spell, though, and woke them up.**

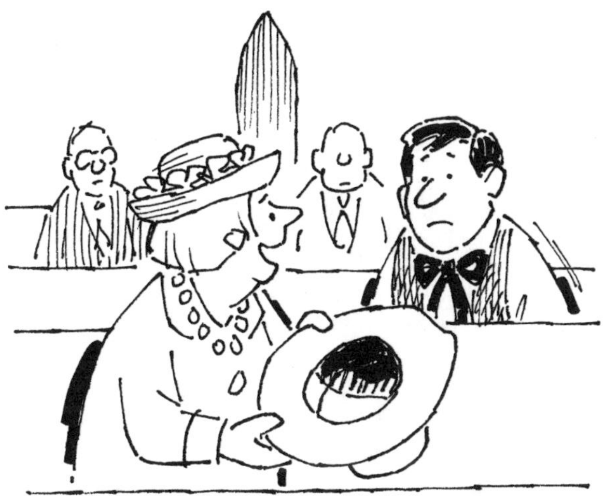

The cowboy leaned over to scratch an itch during a pause in the sermon, and his hat toppled off into the lap of the lady in front of him. She turned to face the embarrassed cowhand and, handing his hat back, graciously inquired, **"Are you taking up your own collection, young man?"**

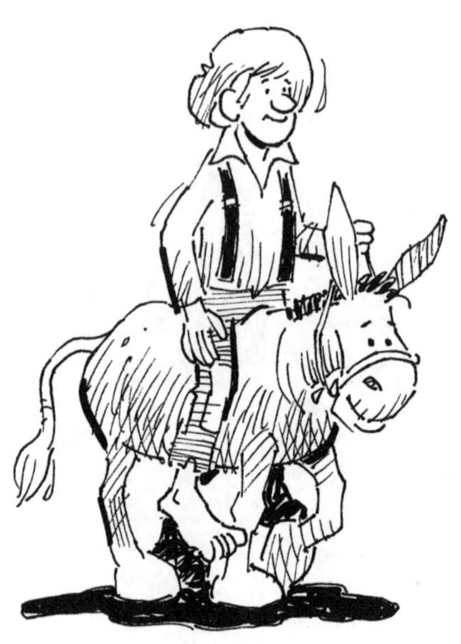

Slim Kaboodle
went to town

Riding on
a jackass.

"Ah, Slim," the
priest said...

**"You weren't here
for Mass."**

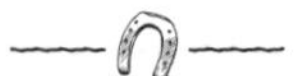

The indigent miner overloaded the TNT blast and was blown to bits. Friends gathered his remains into a hastily built pine box and labeled it, **"Adios, Slim. Rest in pieces."**

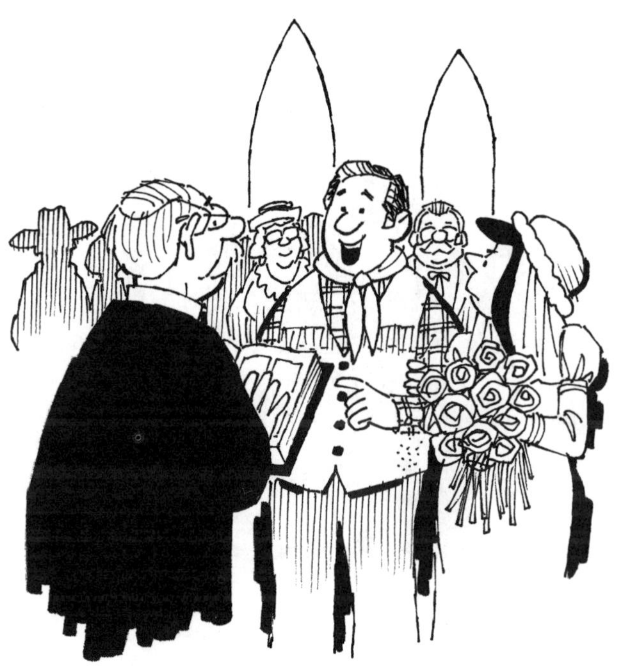

"Funny you should ask that!"

"He ain't much at preaching,
but he's a heck of a fund raiser."

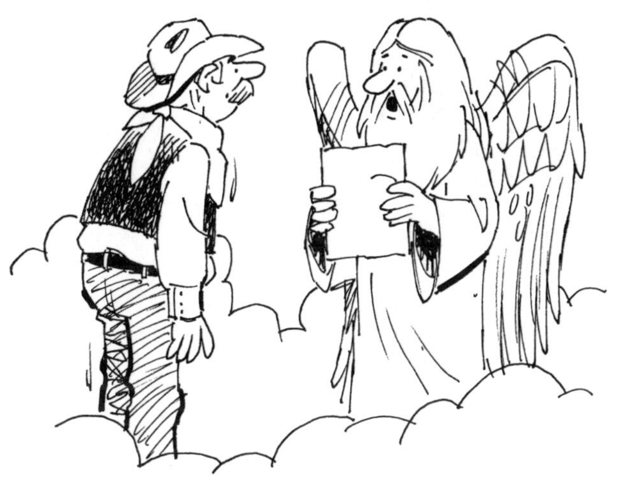

"Smoking or non-smoking?"

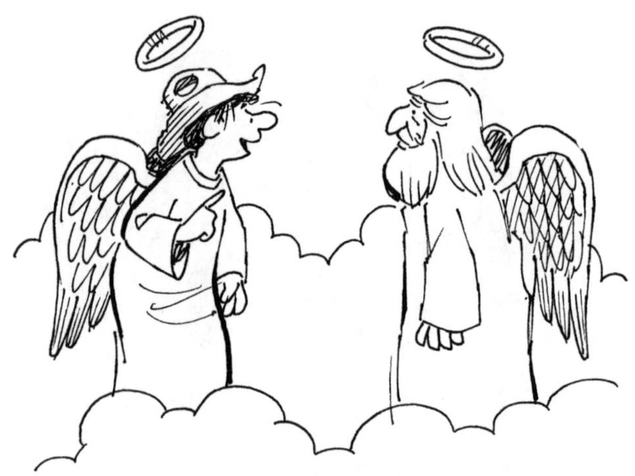

"I ate a plate of our cook's 'Heavenly Stew,' and, sure enough, here I am."

The preacher delivered a forceful sermon. **It forced almost everyone to leave church early.**

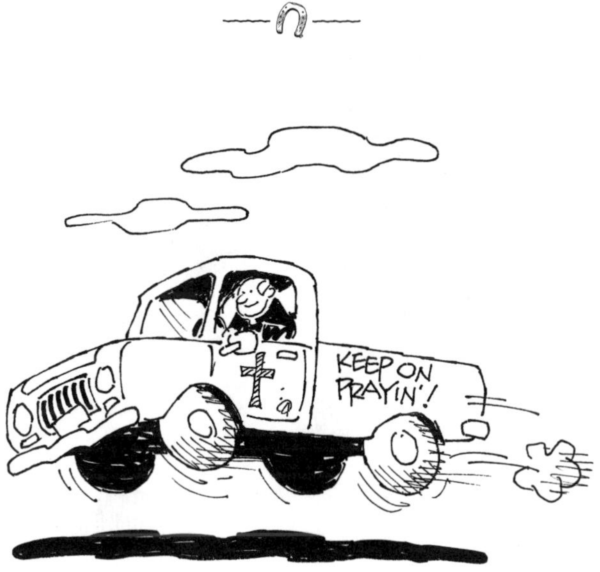

A preacher in a pickup is our kind of preacher.

Don't Ever...

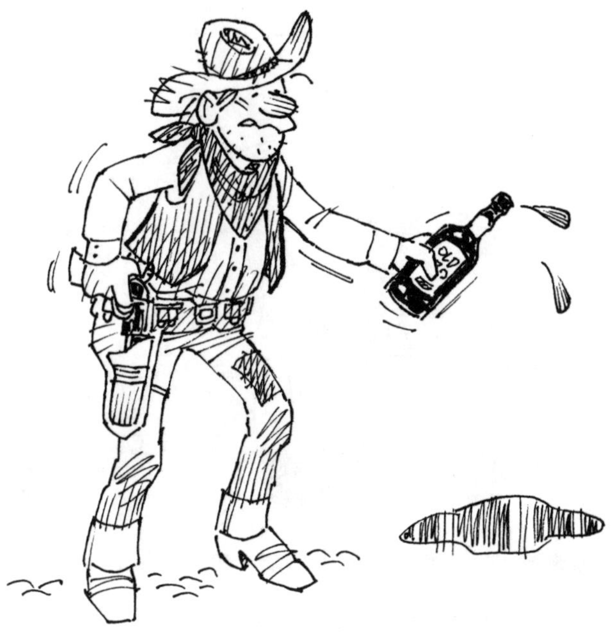

...drink and draw!

Don't ever:

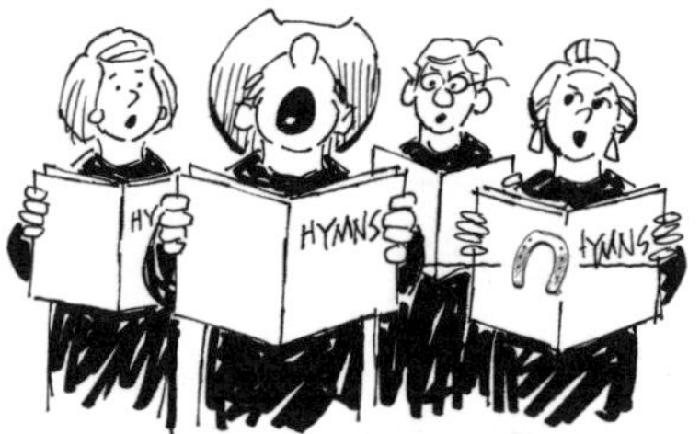

Drown out the rest of the choir, **even if you do think you sound like Tennessee Ernie Ford.**

Wear your hat in church. **Nobody is going to mistake it for a halo.**

Take off your boots in church. **There is no sanctity in smelly socks.**

Say sheep to a cowman. **It could start a war.**

Take difference with the parson. **He has more pull with the man above.**

Don't ever:

Ask a cowboy the 10 questions that most likely will start a fight:

10. Did you ever **date a giraffe**?

9. Do you **cry over spilled beans**?

8. Do you wear **clean underwear every day**?

7. **Didn't you hear me the first time**, dummy?

6. Did you get them clothes **at the Salvation Army**?

5. Do you like **boys or girls best**?

4. Do you always smell like that or are you **just wearing a cheap cologne**?

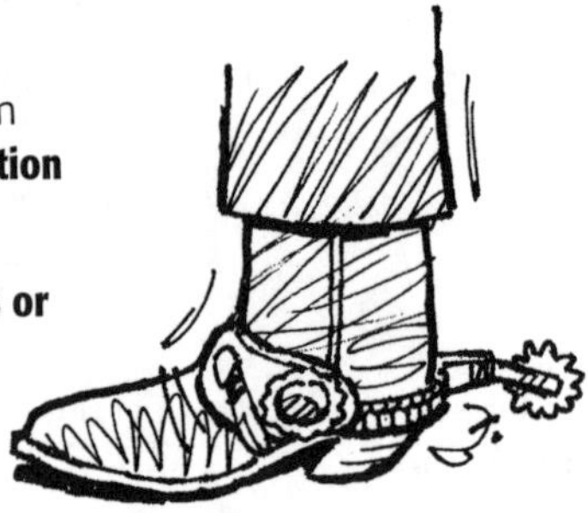

3. What's your opinion of **strangers who ask you what's your opinion**?

2. Didn't you ever **put on a saddle before**?

1. Do you use your bandanna **for a bib**?

Don't ever:

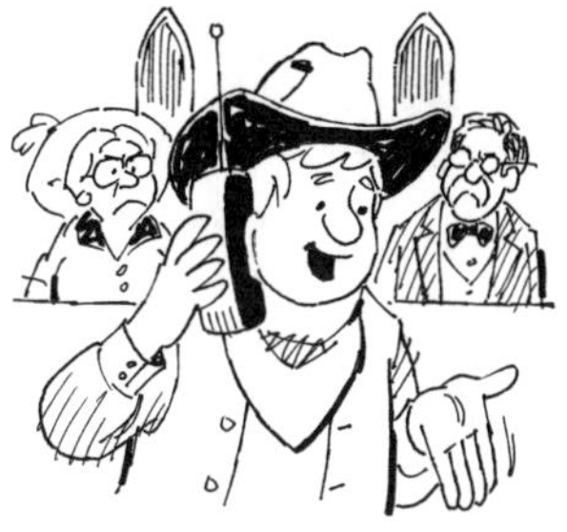

Use your cell phone during the sermon. **It might short-circuit the Good Word.**

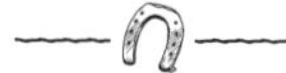

Take your cows **to a horse doctor.**

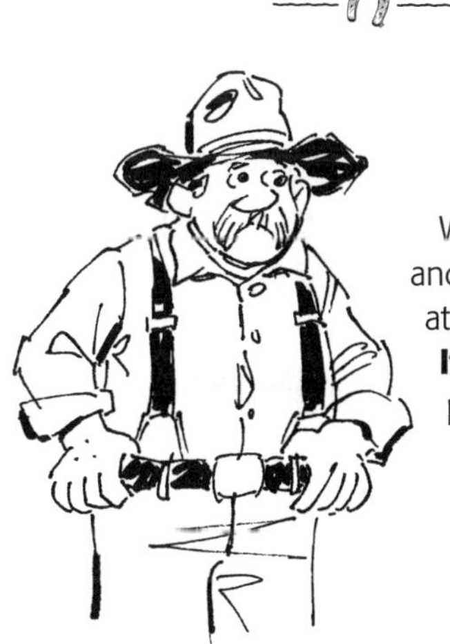

Wear a belt and suspenders at the same time. **It's indicative of paranoia.**

Don't ever:

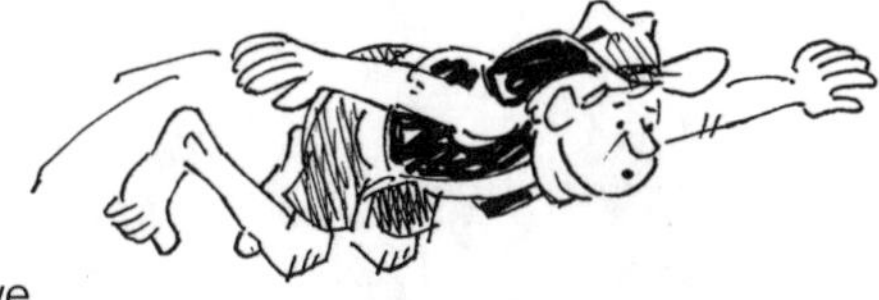

Do a swan dive **into a dry lake.**

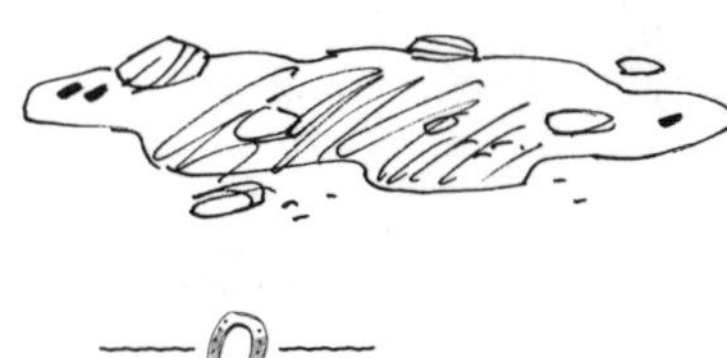

Eat lamb. **It just ain't cowboy.**

Slow dance **at a hoe-down.**

Play a guitar **at a fiddle contest.**

Put **horseshoes on a cow.** (As if you could!)

Don't ever:

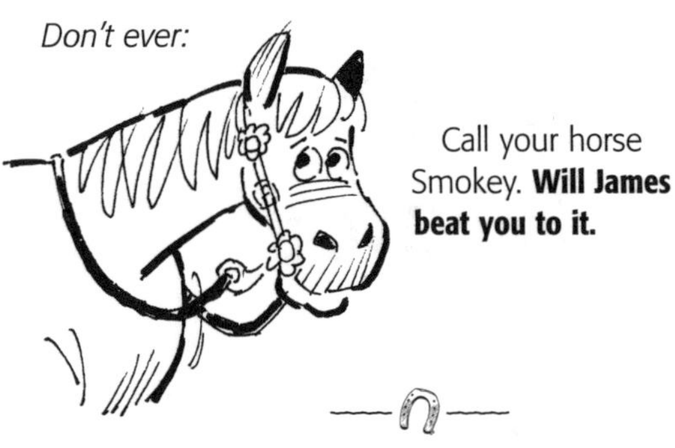

Call your horse Smokey. **Will James beat you to it.**

Rope a calf **with its mama between you and it.**

Mend fence **that ain't broke.**

Try to pitch hay **with a shovel.**

Try to shovel snow **that hasn't fallen.**

Too Much Tabasco?

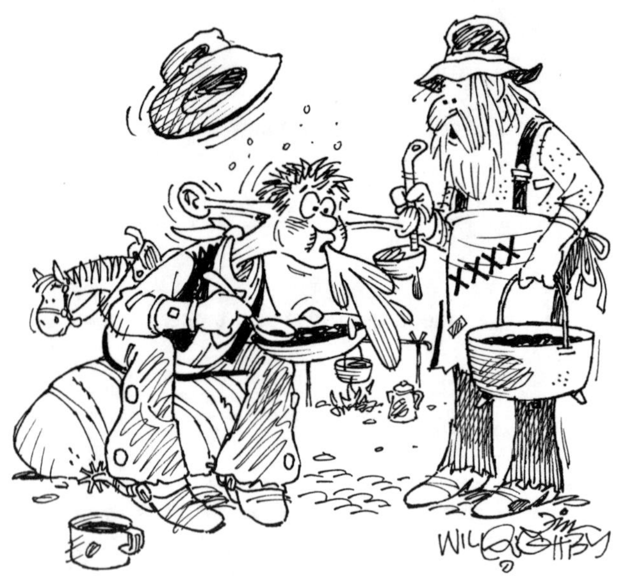

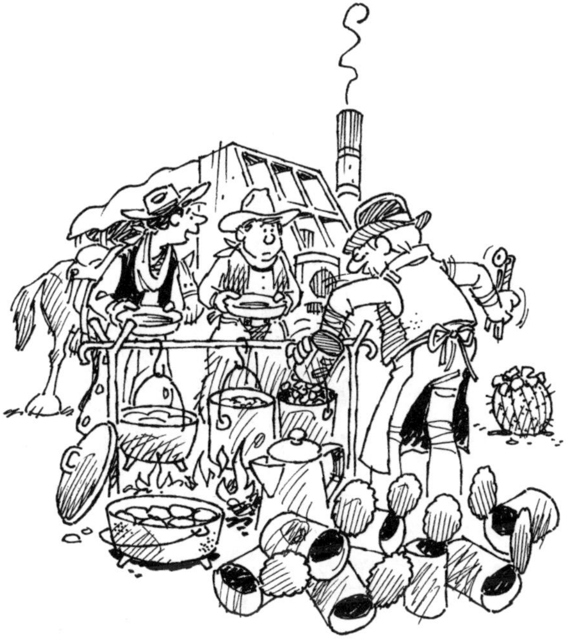

"Without that can opener, he'd never make it as a cook."

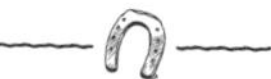

The cowboy sputtered helplessly after eating some of the mystery concoction in front of him. Chuckling, the cook offered, "I call it 'Mule Moutarde'. **That's because of the kick it delivers."**

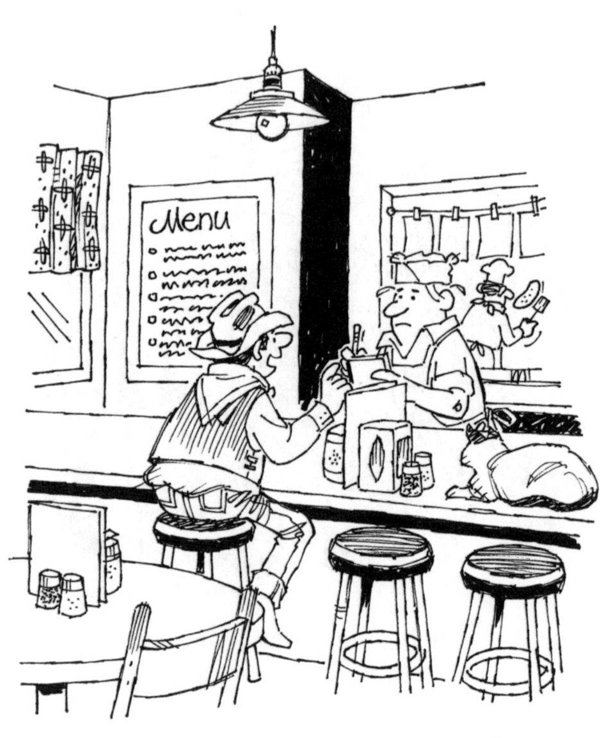

"I'll have your 'cowboy special'."

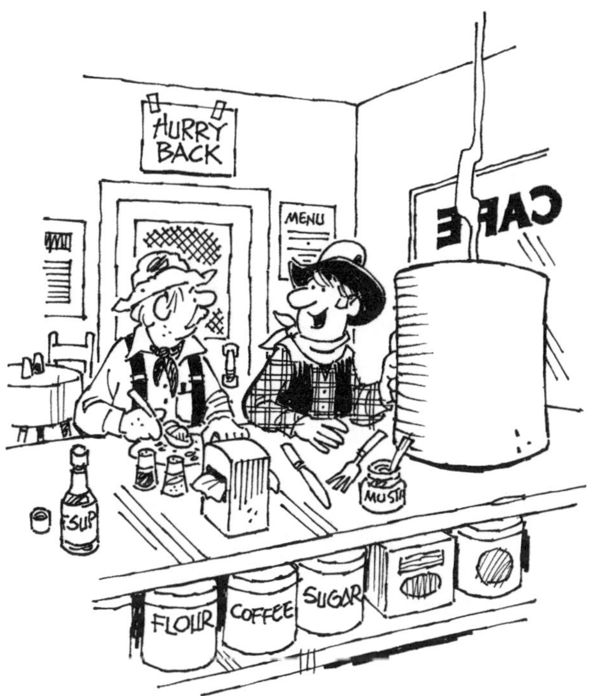

"There's nuthin' like a cup of hot coffee to get you goin' in the morning!"

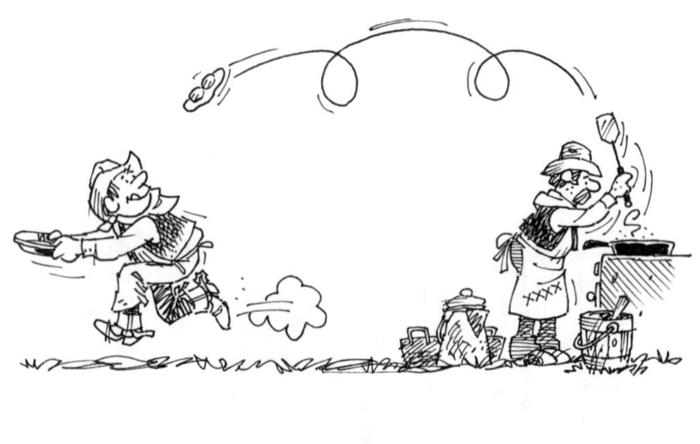

Two cowboys came riding into camp, hungry. "What all have you got to eat?" one asked the cranky cook. "You have two choices," the cook replied. **"Bean casserole or nothing."**

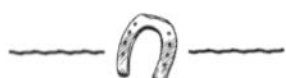

The boys had been razzing the camp cook. He had had about enough when one hand asked for some sugar to stir into his thick, black coffee. The cook clubbed him sharply on the head with a heavy ladle, saying, **"One lump or two?"**

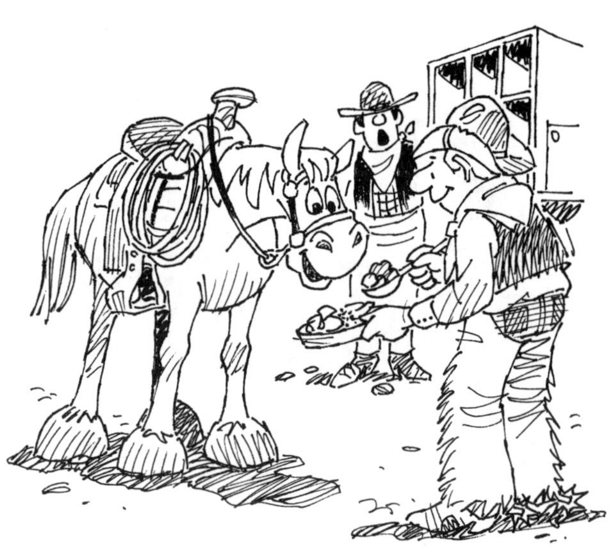

"You're too good to that horse, Hansen!"

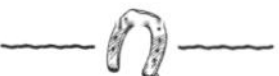

A disgruntled cowhand spewed out a mouthful and addressed the cook with scorn, "This chili tastes like something out of a spittoon."

"Mebbe so," the cook replied, "I ain't never tasted a spittoon's contents."

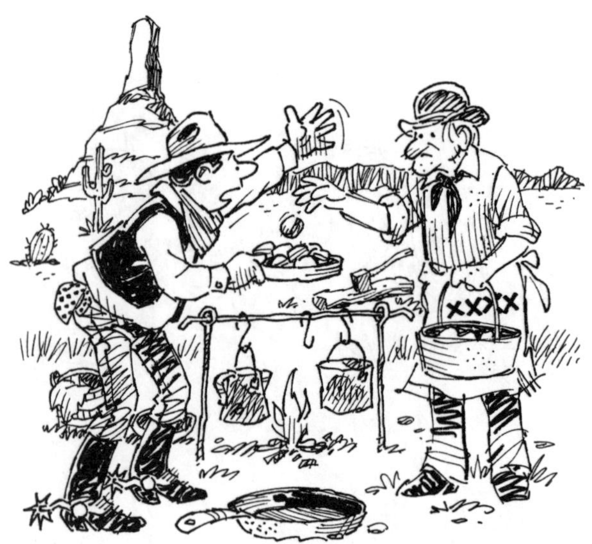

"Man cannot live by biscuits alone!"

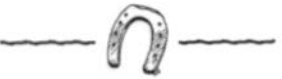

I ain't saying our cook's food is bad, but one day a grubby-looking hobo wandered into camp saying he was dying of hunger. Old Moses quickly dished him up some of that day's ignoble stew and said, "Here, this will sure keep you alive."

Taking two or three hasty mouthfuls, the hobo got wide-eyed, leaned forward, and spit it all out. **"I'd rather die," he muttered.**

When there aren't enough forks to go around, a cowboy will often resort to his fingers. **Using them, not eating them.**

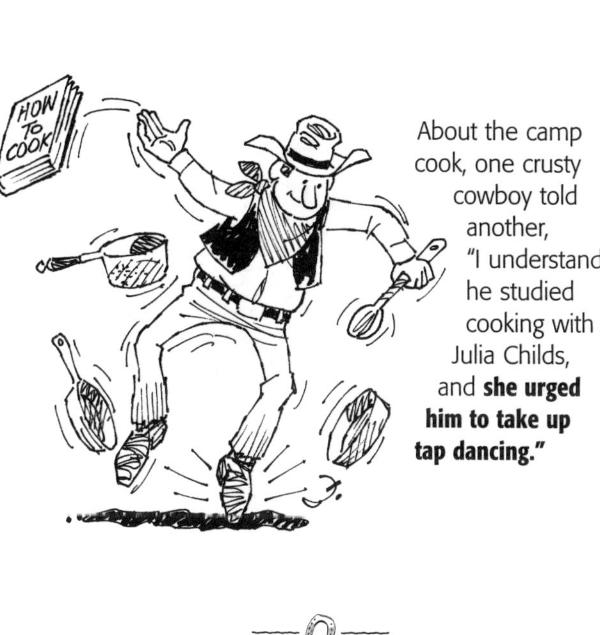

About the camp cook, one crusty cowboy told another, "I understand he studied cooking with Julia Childs, and **she urged him to take up tap dancing."**

A city dude would gag if he knew **what mountain oysters really are.**

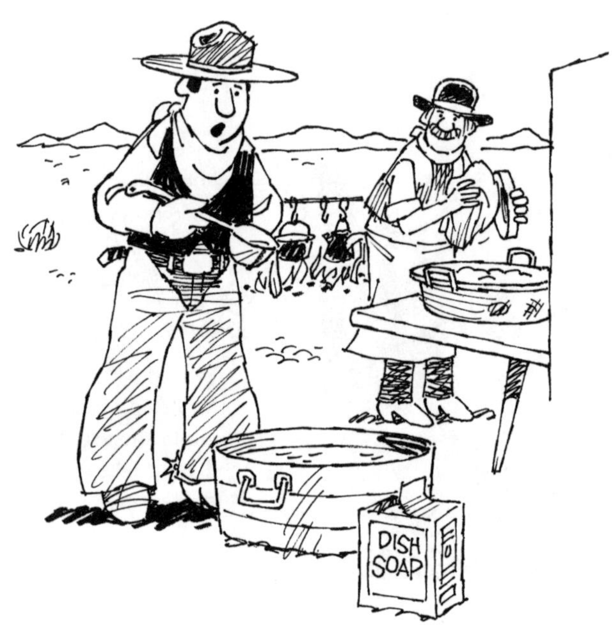

"This water has a funny taste."

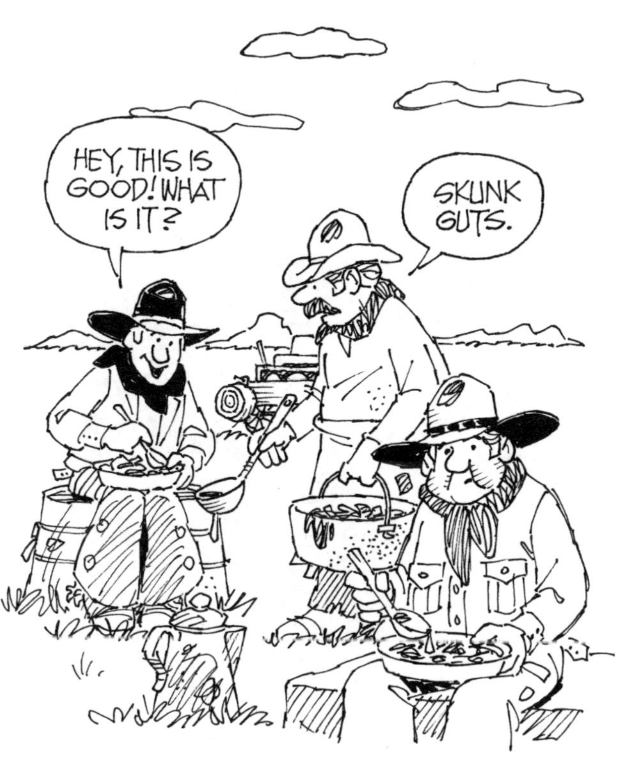
HEY, THIS IS GOOD! WHAT IS IT?
SKUNK GUTS.

It Was the Judge

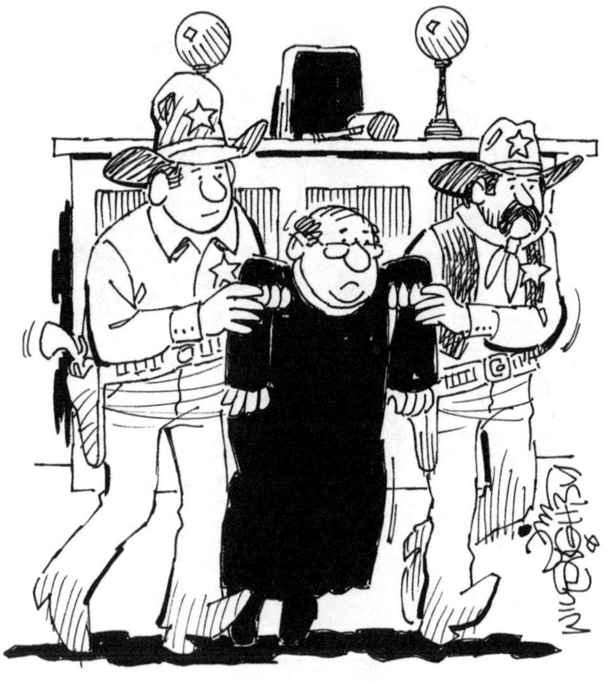

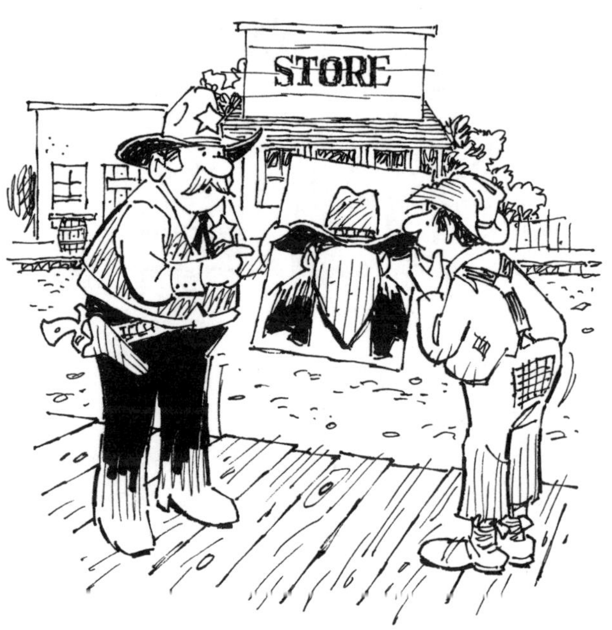

"We're looking for this stagecoach robber. Have you seen him around?"

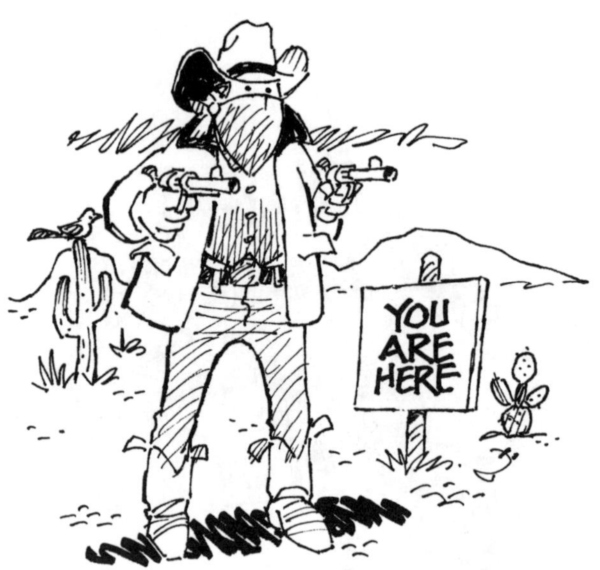

Two seedy-looking bad guys struck up a conversation in a Payson saloon. Asked where he worked, one answered, **"Wherever I happen to be during any given holdup."**

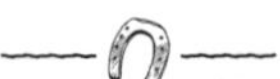

Today, police call for backup to help arrest a jaywalker. In old times, the sheriff moved in and nailed the bad guys with just the help he had on hand, **usually a mere 100-man posse.**

Chasing a band of cattle rustlers, my horse ran so hard, **I got out of breath.**

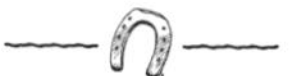

Two rough-looking outlaws dashed out of the Benson Bank, loaded down with bags of loot, only to find their horses missing. **"Dang!" muttered one. "You can't trust anyone anymore."**

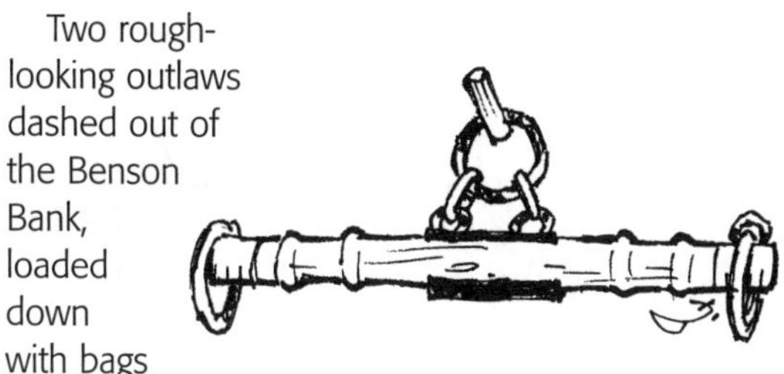

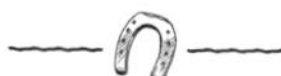

It's good to study under an expert. A cowboy of our acquaintance studied about bank robbing from Jesse James. They made a big haul on the Kingman Bank, rode out of town, and bedded down in a secluded aspen grove, congratulating themselves on a job well done. Next morning, the proud student woke up and found Jesse gone, together with the loot.

It was part of the lesson.

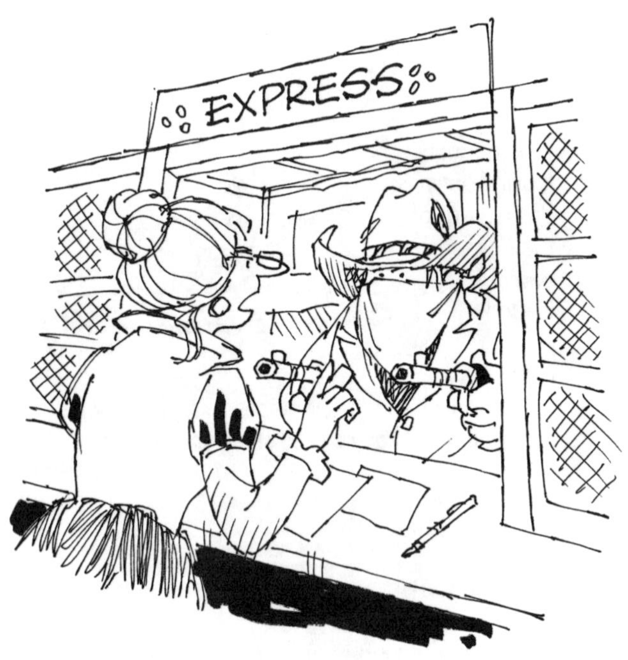

"You'll have to wait in line like everybody else, young man."

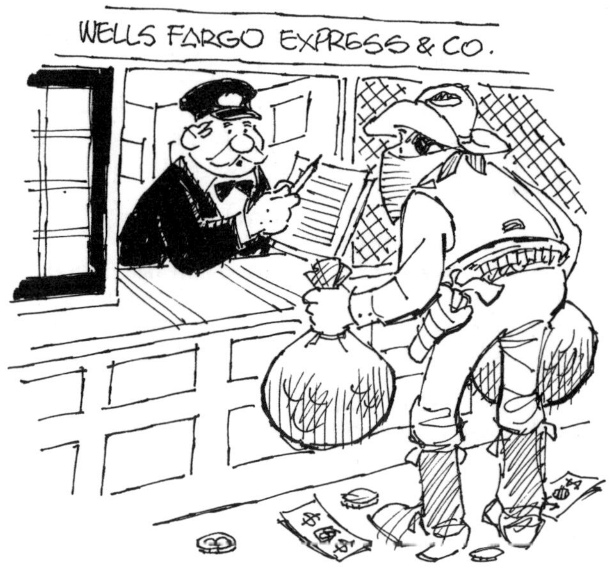

"Now, if you'll just sign these cash transfer forms."

Other Funny Little Books From WitWorks™

Cow Pie Ain't No Dish You Take to the County Fair
Cartoons and jokes churn up fun with cowboy facts of life.
$6.95 #ACWP7

Never Give a Heifer a Bum Steer
Arizona's official historian Marshall Trimble spins tall tales about small-town life.
$7.95 #ANVP9

Growing Older is So Much Fun EVERYBODY'S Doing It
Gene Perret casts a funny glow over senior citizenship.
$6.95 #AGOP0

Someday I Want to Go to All the Places My Luggage Has Been
Gene Perret pokes fun at the things about travel that bug us.
$7.95 #ALLP9

Never Stand Between a Cowboy and His Spittoon
Jokes taken from Territorial newspapers are classy or crass, and they reflect what was funny at the time.
$6.95 #ABLP0

Do You Pray, Duke?
Cowboy-oriented chuckles from cartoonist Jim Willoughby.
$6.95 #ADDP0

Retirement: Twice the Time, Half the Money
Retirees have more time but less money, and Emmy-winner Gene Perret jokes about that condition.
$6.95 #ARTS2

Grandchildren Are So Much Fun We Should Have Had Them First
Doting grandparents. Impish kids. Gene Perret mixes the two into loads of laughs.
$6.95 #AGRS3

HMOs, Home Remedies & Other Medical Jokes
Linda Perret dispenses humor about dealing with insurance companies, being sick, and getting cured.
$6.95 #AHPS3

available in bookstores

To order a book or request a catalog from WitWorks™
call toll-free 1-800-543-5432.
In Phoenix or outside the U.S., call 602-712-2000.
Online at www.witworksbooks.com